the good   **the bad**

the e funny

THE GOOD

THE BAD

THE FUNNY

▽

DE ARCANO NOSTRAE SANCTISSIMAE
MIRABILISQUE TRINITATIS, EIUS POTESTATE
SANANDI ET REDIMENDI VIM STATISTIS -
AD QUAE EXCOGINATIO EIUS CONTRIBU-
TIONIS ULTIMAE AD MAGISTERIUM MAGI-
CAE ARTIS NOSTRAE ADDITA EST

△

Adamai Philotunus

✡

MCMXCII
GLEVUM

The Mouse That Spins

THE GOOD
THE BAD
THE FUNNY

By Adamai Philotunus

Originally published in 1992 by the Mouse That Spins, England, as
edition of about half a dozen copies for friends.

First e-book edition published by El-cheapo
for The Mouse That Spins 2000

First print on demand paperback edition
by The Mouse That Spins, 2002

ISBN: 0-904311-10-4

ISBN 978-0-904311-21-1

E-books available at web-orama.com
books@web-orama.com / publisher@el-cheapo.com

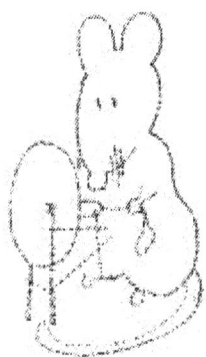

the mouse that spins

CONTENTS

For Alaric

Oh my son, would that it were within my power to bring you up in a better world than that which was mine.

Not that I have reason to complain of my lot, for I have lead a life of as many pleasures, hopes, excitements and satisfactions as of despairs, disappointments and failures. Yet, however good was my world, still would I wish to leave you a better one - for that is Progress. There are those who would insist that "higher" is "better"; adopting that convention, for the time being, I would not just want to lead you to a high place but also one where the path slopes upward with a promise of even better things to come.

Progress, like any deity, responds to worship. Like any deity She is also ready to steal the soul of those who worship Her blindly. Worshipped moderately, however, She responds with the gift of Hope - and that is one quality which does seem to be on the wane at this point on our path, my son.

For I see a world in a state of division. Man not part of Nature, but Her antithesis. Empires crumbling into nations that are themselves entering into civil war. Societies being divided into communities and then broken down into families who own their own homes and their own at-home entertainments; and those families breaking down into individuals who in turn are at war inside themselves. I see bodies in rebellion, growing cancers for their own downfall. I see the immune system - itself the very definition of a body's unique identity - under attack from the virus or whatever entity it is that triggers AIDS.

Addiction brought two souls together: addiction to the Pleasure/Pain torments of Love and Hate. It was within such a maelstrom that you were conceived, my son, defining one very sound reason why I would never wish to banish addiction. I believe mankind is meant to live the torments of Love/Hate, is meant to live the ecstacies as well as the withdrawal horrors of a thousand physical and emotional drugs. My wish is not to cure addiction, but rather to heal it by adding a third principle to the duality to make it whole. Addiction to become a game to play and to abandon, rather than remain itself one dangerously seductive pole of yet another Good/Bad duality. Why should a year exploring the agonies and ecstacies of the heroin experience be any less laudable than a year spent exploring the agonies and ecstacies of walking to the South Pole? Both could destroy, both could illumine. Yes, you were yourself a third principle that was added to our addiction, but the patterns of duality were too well established to save the marriage. What chance has my message to be heard above such din?

Contemplating that previous example: most say that it is the HIV virus that is responsible for the condition called AIDS, but there are some which deny this as a pernicious fallacy - misinformation, in fact. But a malignant virus is itself just a section of DNA containing information which propagates itself at the expense of its host. So both camps would agree that it is misinformation of one type or another that lies behind AIDS and leads to the break up of a human body.

To what extent can we trace all the other ills I have described to the spread of wrong information?

Might not, to the same extent, the spread of different information provide an equally profound and all-pervasive cure for those very ills?

In presenting this book to the world, my son, I am releasing a counter-virus to the virus of Division. Not so much a virus of Unity - which would be the anti-virus to which we are already well immunised by centuries of exposure - as a virus of Flux or Movement. A virus whose objective it is to discourage the crystallising and isolating effects of Division and encourage in their place a sense of flow and adaptation.

For Division is not in itself bad. We are stardust, my son: stars had to be torn apart and separated into atoms to create the dust from which our bodies have been made. Would you, with hindsight, regret the breaking up of those stars?

If the forces which drive us apart are allowed then to hold us apart, then indeed are Progress and Hope banished from our world. But if those forces can surrender power so that movement and flow can take place - then Hope not only survives, She flourishes.

This book then is my gift to the world on your behalf. A virus of Flux which just might transform the war between Unity and Division into a dance.

It might equally be rejected by the remnants of our immune systems: become another cranky little volume safely isolated and contained somewhere in the Copywrite Libraries' shelves. Some would say it is therefore a sorry gift and that I, who failed to combat the virus of Division within mine own family, would do better to work towards giving you some more substantial legacy than this.

But here I am, seated at my trusty old GRiD. Which would you really prefer me to present: the gift of what I have to offer, however small? or a lengthy apology for all that I failed to give you as a father, as a friend, and as a fellow human being?

My name is Adamai Philotunus, born a free citizen of Albion as the smoke of war began to clear over Europe. Like others of my generation I was born into an atmosphere of Hope, dreams of a new beginning, a new society, and find it hard to live without that air to breath. Yet our role is not just to demand hope, but also to bear it within us as a bee secretes honey. Our hope-born generation paid back this investment, this gift of Hope, in the nineteen sixties to the extent that society later felt sickened by its sweetness. Older and wiser, I seek now to present what I have preserved of that Hope for a society which no longer seems to expect it.

I present it in the form of words. "The Good, The Bad, The Funny" or "The Good, The Bad And The Funny"?

The second version sounds better because it resonates in a stranger's mind with the success of a film called "The Good, The Bad And The Ugly". So, under the second title this book might be a little more noticed. However, the addition of "and" serves to put the three concepts into sequence - a beginning, a middle and an end - and that goes against the spirit of the book itself. Without the "and" we have three separate and individual parts which can arrange themselves in any pattern on a page and be taken in any sequence - and that is definitely in keeping with the dancing spirit that invokes this book.

Trying to put ideas into words is tricky and generates many paradoxes. For example: unity is not one-dimensional, it has no dimension; whereas duality is one dimensional, and trinity (the subject of this book) is two dimensional - and that is why those three concepts when deprived of the linking "and" can be placed anywhere on the page. Quaternity should be three dimensional and therefore very powerful in our three dimensional space; however, quaternity is often presented in two dimensions where it loses all its life. Later in this book we will give it the gift of a third dimension and restore it to its rightful heritage.

If I put my ear to the ground I hear a dry, crackling voice say "one, two, four - all at war! one, two, four - all at war" and I know something is sorely missing. I take a cup, pour from it the liquid three and put my ear once more to the ground. "One, two three, four - give us more! give us more!"

Ares was not just the Greek God of War, he was also the God of Dance. In writing about the Trinity I will stick to a book whose pages have four sides, and I will write in one-dimensional sentences with a beginning and an end. I bring to you the number three as a new friend and adviser, not as a usurper to any throne.

This trinity of which I write is but one thing in many. Yet it is an ocean in which all can dwell and it is fed by four great rivers. So that is how we shall approach it: from four directions, beginning with the river which enters it from the West.

PARS UNA

ooooo

DE RE AQUAE

One river flows from the West. It is a river of deepest Water in which I
fear to drown or be devoured by the many biting things that slither in
its depths. Yet a most fecund source it is, and therefore a wise choice for
my first river of approach. Having once braved the river from the West,
its terrors can no more hold me back from this quest.

I was invited to a dinner party in the ancient capital of England. It was a small party around a table where a single conversation could most comfortably prevail. Mine host was expounding his observation that there were two types of men: those who seek women with large breasts and those who seek women with small or negligible breasts.

My mind flickered ahead of the conversation in anticipation, wondering into which category the speaker would put himself. It was through working with his last girlfriend that we had first met: so I conjured her image to my mind for an answer to this speculation.

I saw a bicycle - his girlfriend had recently left the country with the plan to cycle from the very North to the very South of the American continents. Starting from the roadway my inner eye saw plimsolls, white socks and then began the long ascent of a pair of slim, tanned legs, silky in the sunlight which presented their fine blond down as a golden aura. Up, up, past knees and firm thighs to pale blue running shorts moulded to boyish hips... by which time a sort of drunkenness of the senses had overtaken me until I was brought round by the challenge of a direct gaze from a bright, intelligent face framed by short blond hair. That sight was in itself so pleasing that, when I sought to repair my quasi-sensory omission, my downward gaze was again befuddled until brought once more sharply into focus by the vision of those exquisite legs.

So, what about her breasts? And what did they reveal of my host? He was now expanding his thesis to suggest that men can be divided into those motivated by the quest for a mother, and those who rather seek a daughter. The mother-lovers go for the ample bosom while the daughter-lovers prefer a skinny girl with flat chest.

There were murmurs of agreement among those present, but I was still caught in perplexity. So I voiced my confusion, pointing out that I was capable of spending all day in the company of a woman and not, at the end of the day, have any idea at all whether she had big, little or even, maybe, rectangular breasts.

Now it is a fine thing to provide a counter-example for a theory too neat, but unless something positive is added it can be no better than an act of vandalism. The rules of play, and the rules of politeness, prefer that we put forward an alternative to be demolished in its turn.

So I suggested that men could instead be divided into those who sought women with legs, and those who preferred them without legs. To save possible misunderstanding I qualified this by explaining that some women, whatever their actual physical attributes, adopted a style that seemed to go shimmery below the waist like a mermaid. Such women probably wore long skirts and you could describe them as witches, or as melusines, for their pose was as strange creatures who never looked you directly in the eye. Whereas there were other women who seemingly flaunted very definite and purposeful legs - especially when in trousers or short skirts, but even when wearing long dresses. Women assuming this role would look you straight in the eye with a challenging gaze and could be described as amazons.

I suggested that some men had insufficient mystery in their lives, and so they sought it by pursuing women of mystery. While other men had as much or more mystery as they could handle, and so they sought the support and partnership of a champion, or at least an equal companion, in the form of an amazon.

So often out of kilter with my environment, I expected a puzzled silence, laughter or a change of topic. To my surprise and relief the man opposite me thoughtfully agreed. I glanced at his wife: even through the dining table's inch of solid British oak I could clearly see legs. They were written all over her.

Please, kind reader, do not despise our small talk. Nations have gone to war over far more trivial matters than these. Had history taken a different course, without my contribution to the conversation, our host (who was a public speaker) could have taken up the cause. By now our streets might be filled with rubble and smoke like some East European melting pot; barricades and burning cars over which might flutter tatty banners reading "Whoppers" or "Flatties" depending which side the bearer was on.

Of course, mine own contribution might have altered no more than the title of the war: the same people could end up fighting under the headings of "Tits" versus "Legs". Or, had my version totally swamped mine host's argument, the war might have been polarised under banners reading "Amazons" and ... well, shall we say "Swallows"?

But none of that happened. His two-fold scheme:-

Tits $\longleftrightarrow$ No Tits

met a second two-fold scheme:-

Legs ⟵⟶ No Legs

and out of it was born a four fold scheme:-

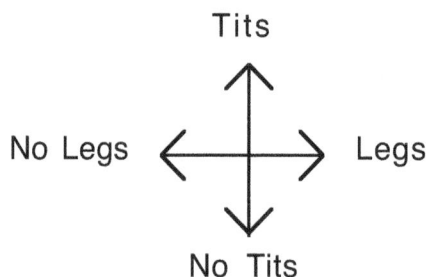

Tits

No Legs ⟵⟶ Legs

No Tits

which suggested that men have in their subconscious minds a compass with which to keep their bearings while exploring the wild and confusing ocean of womanhood. That compass has four directions which are labelled not by words but by goddess images which I can only suggest by the four labels: Mother, Daughter, Amazon and Witch.

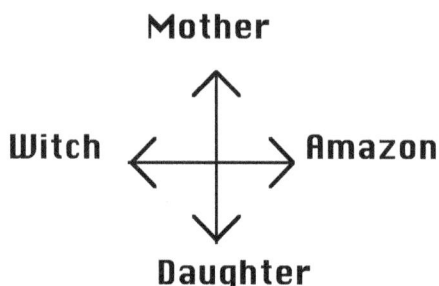

Mother

Witch ⟵⟶ **Amazon**

Daughter

Most difficult is that last label, because it is a word which is for certain people intensely negative in its associations. Yet that fact too has its place in the order of things, because each of these four goddesses has her pleasant and unpleasant aspects, and the fear in the word "witch" is merely an incomplete (rather than an inappropriate) association for the mystery woman of no legs.

Putting this all together, I could feel very proud of my contribution because it had diverted a potential conflict. People go to war over two-fold divisions but not over four-fold divisions. Four is not the number of war, so much as the number of analysis.

Do I therefore hear the applause of my readers resounding in my ears? Maybe... but also maybe not. Because some people might be merely irritated by my apparent typecasting of women.

Now the funny thing is that I my endeavour was not to typecast women, but rather to present the image of a compass with which men can plot a course. There is no place called "North" just as there is no woman called "Amazon", however much some show aspects of that image. Yet, were I to stop my writing here and say no more, I bet that most of my readers would in a few days only recall something about my having "defined four types of women".

You see, just as the tendency of a two-fold division is for it to degenerate into war, so the tendency of a four fold division is for it to crystallise in our minds into "types". Many are they who have wrestled with Jung's four types, trying to see where themselves and their friends fit. Even in the case of a well-used and clearly understood concept like the four points of a compass, you still find people debating whether, say, Gloucester belongs in "the South West" or whether Derby is a "Northern" town; and they do so in a way which suggests that the points of the compass have in their thoughts lost their flexibility as a navigational aid and crystallised into clear categories or "types".

There is an innate dissatisfaction about typecasting. Find any popular description of types - the Sloane Ranger versus the Essex Man, let us say - and most people cannot resist analysing themselves and others on these lines; but as soon as the table is turned and others start to analyse *them* on such a scheme it becomes offensive and they rebel against "typecasting". This rebellion is very severe: if I had said no more than the fact that my friend had described two types of men, those who went for big tits and those who went for small tits, then I predict that some readers would have reacted angrily by saying that it was sexist to "classify women in this way", even though the true object of his classification had not been women, but rather men.

Why are we so sensitive about typecasting? One reason is that, although the nature of a fourfold division is analytical and not combative, when it is presented as a two dimensional scheme - as a cross with four arms - it invariably breaks into two pairs of opposites. We hear of "the North/South divide" or the "East/West conflict", but never of the "North South East West" conflict or divide.

That is one reason why we object to analysis, maybe, but I would suggest that there is another more subtle reason. So subtle in fact that I will require all of this book to argue that it is so. My belief is that the progression from two fold to four fold thinking - although definite progress in so far as it replaces conflict with thoughtful analysis - can be unsatisfying because it bypasses a

deep and unacknowledged hunger for three-fold thinking.

I will not argue that three-fold thinking is "better" in any absolute sense, but I will argue that it provides
something lacking in the respective simple and refined
dualities of two and four-fold thinking. Water is not
nutritionally superior to dried peas, but it is what the
desert survivor most desperately needs.

What, then, is this three-fold thinking? I do not
know. Let us find out together in this book. Sufficient
now to say that I went home from that dinner party with
a puzzle in my mind: my four-fold scheme had revealed
four faces of the Goddess - but isn't She usually described
as having just three faces?

I had described the archetypal woman as Amazon,
Witch, Mother and Daughter. What about those who
describe her as Maiden, Mother and Crone?

Well, you might say, Mother is obviously Mother
and Maiden seems to fit Daughter well enough. So is the
Witch another name for the Crone? You might think so
except that I did present my reservations about using the
word "witch" earlier - for the witch I picture can be young
or timeless, she does not have to be an old woman of
warty chin and hairy nose. What then of the Amazon? Is
she just an additional face tacked on by the male imagination projecting his own essence onto the Goddess? Or
is she another aspect of the Maiden?

What I am here pretending to do is to place my
fourfold scheme over the three-fold scheme in order to
make it fit as best I can. Seeing it, perhaps, as a sort of
refinement or improvement of the three-fold scheme

9

because it has an additional aspect, and greater structure because it contains two pairs of opposites.

This, I will argue, is a mistake; because I have learnt to see four as qualitatively as well as quantitatively different from three. The Book Of The Law states that "all numbers are infinite", suggesting that there are indeed other, non quantitative ways to distinguish them.

The four-fold and the three-fold descriptions of the goddess are both complete and satisfactory in themselves, but they are both saying something different. One is not a subset of the other.

I would like to tell you the difference now and get on with the book. This is, however, the tenth book that I have written, and I have learnt enough to know that publishers like to have any argument flabbed out with lengthy examples and material which would be perfectly easily found in books already produced by other publishers. I have also learnt that it is no good being highty-toighty about this and refusing to go along with it, because readers get used to the environment they are brought up in, so that a book which defies convention can simply cause confusion. Anyway, I am my own publisher and I am now ordering the writer to waffle on a bit about the many faces of the Goddess. At least it gives me an excuse to get up and go for a browse in my library for inspiration. What's more, I will be referring back to the types I define as examples in a later section of this book.

THE MOTHER

"There, Dear, that'll make you feel better".

You open your eyes and prop yourself up with your pillow. There is a cup of tea, of *consommé*, a piece of toast... whatever is the one thing you really want as you recover from your 'flu. Beyond it is a warm, sympathetic face. And now a hand reaches out and smooths your fevered brow.

It's all so lovely that you begin to wonder whether being in bed with 'flu isn't actually nicer than being up and well - and that is a problem with the Mother as type. Whereas a real mother knows her child must eventually become independent, the Mother type is an eternal mother wanting an eternal child. So, although she can be hugely supportive and helpful, it is the sort of help which leads towards increasing dependence upon her to whom mother/child relationship is the real objective.

If you are feeling emotionally insecure, no-one can be more helpful than the Mother type. Talk about problems at work, or with personal relationships, and she will give you the feeling that you alone are in the right and that everyone else must be crooked or barmy. Pressures will be taken off you because she will work very hard on your behalf, cooking meals, mending clothes... all the typically motherly things but also anything else that really helps.

The problem arises, however, if you approach the Mother not from emotional need so much as practical need. Let us say you are no good at keeping your accounts, and there is a Mother type who is good at it. If you have a big inferiority thing about this weakness and break down in tears at your incompetence, then the Mother will take you in her arms and help you with your accounts in such a way that you end up feeling really good about it. If, however, you simply want someone else to do your accounts so that you can get on with more urgent work, it is disastrous to ask the Mother type because her help, however good, is highly interactive. "Where did you say you kept the invoices? Oh, yes, right under my nose!"; "remind me, how do you spell 'sincerely'?"; "come here a minute, darling, I can't read your writing"; "dear me, what a way to file receipts, how on earth do you manage?" and so on and so forth until you realise that you are being kept so busy answering questions and flapping about that it would have been simpler and no less time-consuming just to have done the job yourself.

THE AMAZON

"God, you have got yourself into a pickle, you silly chump. Come on, give it here!"

When it comes to offering support, the Amazon is every bit as tireless as the Mother. If your real need is practical support, she is far better than the Mother. Ask the Amazon to help with your accounts and she would simply do them. A short briefing session to tell her where everything is, then she would banish you from the office having ordered you to bring sandwiches for lunch - and you really would be left free to get on with the other work.

If, however, you were actually feeling emotionally insecure about your inability to manage accounts, then the Amazon has nothing to offer. By the time she has breezed through the job you will be feeling even more of a wimp. You will feel that the only use Life has for you is to bring coffee and sandwiches to serve Superwoman.

Because I am fonder of the Amazon it is harder for me to see the fault, but perhaps it is this. Both the Mother's and the Amazon's help can lead to a state of dependence - it is possible for the Amazon to be so competent that you feel like leaving absolutely everything to her. And yet I do not see that as intrinsic to the type, because the Amazon is not really interested in relationship so much as getting things done - whereas for the Mother getting things done is really a means towards reinforcing a relationship. The Amazon would really be happy to teach you all she knows in order that you could get it done yourself - but again, don't ask her teaching to support your ego if what you really need is an injection of confidence.

The Amazon's manner seems bold and challenging - she stares directly into your eyes because she wants a clear answer, not because she wishes to make eye contact. She is a busy and active person, probably athletic, and that could be why her symbol seems to be legs just as much as breasts are a Mother's symbol. If a child's mother is indeed a Mother type, then its cries for help will be answered by Mother picking it up and hugging it. So in these formative years the constantly reinforced experience of womanhood is of contact with female breasts. But if the mother is an Amazon type she will probably have her hands full or busy, and the child will only be able to reach for her legs. To this child the constantly reinforced image of womanhood is of legs towering overhead - pillars to the temple of a mighty goddess whose upper parts are obscured from the child's upward gaze. Paradoxically a child clinging to one's legs can be even more restricting than a child in one's arms, so the Amazon mother is probably forever having to disentangle the child to restore her freedom of movement, and thereby reinforcing the child's sense of her divine inaccessibility. Thus it is that those who adore the Amazon tend to be worshippers of her type and take her scorn or rejection as a sacrament.

I wonder whether in Red Indian culture, where busy working women carried their babies in papoose backpacks, if the image of the Amazon is not so much of legs as of shoulders?

THE DAUGHTER

"Oh this is so boring. Why can't you just let go and have some fun!"

The sulky pout, the teasing toss of the head... suddenly you look at yourself and realise that you are a bit boring. Funny, you always used to feel a bit of a raver. Now, in the presence of this delicious butterfly of a woman you feel like some dry old stick-in-the-mud. What has happened?

Not like the Mother or the Amazon, there's no point in asking the Daughter for help with anything unless it is frightfully amusing and such fun that you would really like to do it yourself. In fact I find it hard to put in a good word for the daughter until she is gone... then suddenly the world seems a grey and colourless place and you are left sighing with nostalgia for the fun and silly things you did together.

The problem I see with the Daughter is that, like the Mother, she has an underlying objective to establish a relationship. Whereas the Mother seeks to make you dependent and her the provider, the daughter seeks to make you the provider while she is dependent.

As with the Amazon, the daughter can be dangerous if approached from emotional insecurity. If your insecurity is with finance and practical matters then the Amazon can help, but certainly not the Daughter because she will ruin you. The only sort of insecurity the Daughter can help with is intellectual insecurity - she will reassure you with the belief that clear thinking and intellectual ability is all just fuddy-duddy left brain nonsense.

Take my opening illustration: imagine a rather shy and socially awkward introvert. If totally into that role, there is no problem; but if there is an inner raver seeking expression then the person has probably adopted an unconventional manner, exhibiting a certain spontaneity and apparent gayness. When such a person meets the Daughter type he is captivated because she manifests in apparent naturalness all he is striving to cultivate. He imagines that she will help to draw out his inner raver and together they will be "fun people".

What in fact happens is that he is faced with such a torrent of unpredictable, inconsequential irresponsibility that he is thrown back onto his own reliability and carefulness simply to preserve something, even if only a memory of the experience. Whatever gay naturalness had been in his character seems to dry up because he is being mysteriously forced into taking responsibility. The Daughter is moulding him into a father rather than into the wild child he wanted to become - and the pain of it is that she is creating a father in order to provide something she can herself rebel against. He who had began to be proud of his informal freedoms is suddenly being accused of being a boring old fart, and he begins to believe it. Unless you really are a rock solid, dependable and financially secure figure, be careful of the Daughter type because she is a spirit of change and insecurity.

Daughters, apart from having small breasts, can be leggy - but the legs are more of an adornment for slinging over the arms of sofas. They are not purposeful motive machines like the legs of an Amazon.

THE WITCH

"Mmm... I wonder what made you say that?"

The Witch looks at you sideways with half closed eyes and you ignore her question because there is something in her manner that suggests she not only knows the answer already but she probably had it all worked out beforehand and could have predicted your exact words anyway.

I am happy with the word "Witch" because I have had positive experience of real witches, but for many the word is wrong because it is associated with something evil, or something old and ugly. "Priestess" is another suitable word for this type, but again the religious connotations are too strong for some people. "Wise Woman" is very good, except that people again associate wisdom with old age. "Woman of Mystery" is better in this respect, but it is not so neat.

The Witch is as elusive as the Daughter but, whereas the latter seems merely fickle, the Witch type seems to be obeying strict rules which happen to lie outside human comprehension. There is a definite sense of purpose, as with the Amazon, but it is a purpose too strange and subtle to divine.

I have suggested that manipulation can be a problem with the Mother and the Daughter, because both need to establish a sort of relationship, whereas it isn't any problem with the Amazon who would bully rather than manipulate. Funnily enough, it isn't really a problem with the Witch either, because the Witch is so heavily into manipulation.

Whereas the manipulation of the Mother and the Daughter can feel like a sort of underlying rot or poison which spoils the outer benefit, the manipulation of the Witch is out and out what it's all about. To be manipulated by her is not a worrying side effect, but rather the pleasure that one imagines a car must feel when in the hands of a master driver. The Witch can be as hopeless at certain tasks as the Daughter, and both will get others to do the work. With the Daughter one feels exploited, but gains a father's satisfaction for it. With the Witch you do not feel exploited so much as inspired to action.

The gift of the Witch is more spiritual than emotional, intellectual or practical. If your life lacks meaning she will study her crystal ball or read the tarot and tell you of past lives and deep currents of being. With so much on your mind you will be quite unaware of the time it is taking to repair her car or reroof the meditation room.

THE MALE TYPES

Everything I attempt has a direct bearing on this book's thesis in a way that will make more sense if you look back or re-read the text later. Remember we began with a dis-

cussion of types of men, based upon what they were looking for or attracted to. Exploring that topic has lead to me
apparently defining four types of women.

Underlying the argument is a duality -
male/female - and when there is an underlying duality I
believe that any attempt to work on one side tends to produce an equal and opposite reaction on the other side. You
set out to crush a communist revolution, and the action of
your soldiers just precipitates the revolution. I try to clarify the desires of men by analysis and I find four women
pinned to my dissecting table.

This book aims to transcend this dualist trap (not
eliminate it) but until that is achieved I had better balance
my work by pointing out that there are four male equiva-
lents to the four female types described.

The Father is the great provider, like the Mother.
Typified by a sort of pipe-smoking conservative Volvo
owner, he has a special relationship as provider for the
Daughter. This can be a very good and stable relationship
unless his attraction to the daughter is an addictive compensation for his own unexpressed Boy.

The Boy is a fickle being like the Daughter. He
tends to be too brilliant for his own good, full of ideas that
never get put into practice. He can form a good relationship with a Mother, but unfortunately one Mother is
never enough because he does not have the basic relationship need that is more obvious in the Daughter. Fine for
him, but agony for the Mother who waits at home.

The Hero or Warrior is a man of action. More a
creature of blind force than the Amazon who shows
greater intellectual and practical ability. He is like an

engine that needs the Witch to direct him because, unless given some "cause" or meaning in life, he can be just a violent trouble maker.

The Priest or Poet is the counterpart of the Witch. A sense of great wisdom and knowing. Unlike the Witch whose wisdom is unfathomable and incommunicable, this wise man can give his teachings as a guru, or present his work as an artist. He tends to revere the Amazon who, although the epitome of strapping femininity in his eyes, somehow manages the trick of also being "more of a man" and so utterly unattainably divine. John Betjeman in his poem "The Olympic Girl" ("fair tigress of the tennis courts, so short in sleeve, so strong in shorts") asks:

"Is it distaste that makes her frown,
So furious and freckled, down
On an unhealthy worm like me?"
    and *"Would I were...*
An object fit to claim her look."

REAL PEOPLE

I remind you that these types are just images, not real people. I do that not in order to trash what will, I hope, prove a useful exercise, but rather so that we can watch very carefully what happens as the book progresses.

Real people are in fact most complex and confusing. All types dwell as potential in all people. If we take no more than the combination of Mother and Amazon we find a woman who will provide a lot of "motherly" domestic services: the question then would be to what extent does her action serve to free you in accordance with the Amazon nature, or to what extent does, say, care for your socks become a major dependency issue ("did you put on the socks I repaired yesterday, not those horrible spotted things - really, you cannot expect a client to respect you in those - and are you sure you packed a spare pair... no wait, I'm going to check... what would you do with out me?")

Add the other types in varying proportions to that mix and you begin to wonder what the point of the exercise could be when its actual application turns out to be so confusing. People love to read descriptions of types, but they react with anger at being typecast.

Not that I am blameless. As already stated, my intention is not to provide another jokey men's guide to the fair sex - a neat little set of stereotypes into which tiresome women friends can be packaged and put away safely - and yet it is hard to see the difference between that and what I have written.

Although I have suggested that fourfold descriptions are more analytical than combative, I could not help but slip into dualistic pairing as a technique for defining the types. I contrasted the Amazon's support - which encourages independence and strength - with the Mother's which leads to dependency and weakness. I did that to make a particular point, but realise that it is not altogether fair. A real mother reading that might say I have no right to criticise mothers that way - "it's all very well for you who have never had to bear a child" - and take personally what was meant to be an abstract exercise (even if it did wobble a bit near to reality from time to time).

One instinct in me is to turn back and try a bit harder. Perhaps that bit about the Mother was a bit unfair, should I add another sentence to qualify it? However, experience suggests that any attempt to amplify will only add more words and possibly get me into even deeper waters and greater misunderstanding.

I suspect that disagreement and opposition is unavoidable because of the nature of fourfold thinking and our reaction to it: we see it as pairs of dualities; duality is of its essence; our own thinking is so dualistic that it will automatically want to take sides whenever an opportunity such as this is presented.

Again I ask: is there another way of thinking that would flow more easily without splitting everything up?

THE TRIPLE GODDESS

I was on secure ground in the last section describing those types: trained as an analyst, I find it easy to draw distinctions and present contrasts. Describing the triple Goddess is not so easy.

There is a strong tradition in many cultures of a Great Goddess who is in a sense threefold. Sometimes this is represented by three apparently distinct Goddesses who form a unit: for example, the three Furies, the three Sirens and or the three Fates of ancient Greece. Elsewhere this is represented by one Goddess with three faces or aspects: Artemis as Virgin, Mother and Crone; the Moon as waxing, full and waning; the woman as virgin, mother and whore.

Taking her three faces as Maiden, Mother and Crone, I first have to realise that we are not just dealing with a less sophisticated version of what has gone before. It is no good equating the two schemes by saying Maiden is Daughter, Mother is Mother and Crone is Witch - and the Amazon has been overlooked or is just another aspect of the Maiden. Something different is being indicated here.

For a start we have a greater emphasis on the three parts being of one whole. When I was describing the four-fold scheme, even though I paid lip-service to the idea that all women contain all of the four types in various degrees, it is natural to begin to see the various types as dominant in certain women and so slide into typecasting. Whereas the threefold division is more often described in terms of aspects than types - "the Mother aspect of the Goddess". So, however well intentioned our initial analysis, the fourfold scheme does encourage us to describe people as "the Mother type" whereas the threefold scheme encourages us to say things like "she is playing the Mother", or "she is getting into her Mother aspect". That is rather nicer than typecasting because it suggests a fully formed human being who has a choice of roles, whereas typecasting suggests a less complete being who is cast into one particular role.

But there is another feature which often shows in this three-fold scheme, and that is an element of time. Whereas the Amazon/Daughter/Mother/Witch scheme described four types which could be of any age, Maiden/Mother/Crone can be seen as the life cycle of one woman - first the young girl, who then grows into the full bloom of motherhood, and then shrinks into old age as the Crone. Often there is an additional hint of cyclic rather than linear time: the Crone who dies to be reborn as the Maiden. This is most obvious in the symbolism of the three-fold Moon Goddess who is the Maiden or Artemis when waxing, the Mother or Hera when full, and the Hag or Hecate when waning - only to be "reborn" at the New Moon and the cycle starts again.

Those two features - an underlying unity behind the three aspects, and a sense of cyclic time which allows one aspect to flow into the other - I believe to be most important clues as to the nature of three-fold thinking. Even though we may find three-fold schemes which seem to break those rules.

As a source of examples I take Adam McLean's book "The Triple Goddess" subtitled "An Exploration of the Archetypal Feminine".

In the introduction the author shares my conviction that there is something important to be learnt from the triple Goddess, and that it has something to do with solving the problems inherent in dualistic thinking. "We will come to value a consciousness of cyclical change within ourselves" he writes, and this is exactly what I will be advocating later in this book.

Elsewhere he speaks of "the awful disease of dualism" and describes how a patriarchal system repressed or denied the Goddess and lead to "rigid one-dimensional thinking". Although I agree with much of the spirit of such passages, I still find myself beginning to protest and take sides. Even though his is an account of the Goddess in her triple nature, and is therefore a sort of hymn to non-dualism - I suspect that readers may find it every bit as provocative as my fourfold analysis of female types. I fear that his description of patriarchal repression could divide readers into those who side with him against such repression and those who reject his account as feminist ball-bashing prejudice. If I am right about this reaction it would seem to contradict my claim that three-fold thinking does not have the divisive, combative effects of dualistic or fourfold thinking. So what has gone wrong?

It is surely this: although Adam McLean has written an excellent introduction to the non-dualistic three-fold Goddess, he has unwittingly given his account a dualistic framework by basing it on the idea of patriarchal versus matriarchal traditions. Just as my attempt at uncontroversial, academic four-fold analysis of human nature turned out to be highly contentious because of a strongly dualistic thread running through it, so has McLean's exercise in resolving dualism by introducing us to the Triple Goddess degenerated into a potential battle of the spiritual sexes.

We both set out to transcend dualism, and both end up its victim. I suggest that this is because dualism is deeply part of our nature - it is not a disease to be transcended by trinitarian thinking but rather a valid system of thought which simply needs the balance, or rather the flux, of trinitarian thinking to keep it operating in a healthy manner. Later in this book I will explore the extent to which my trinitarian principle is the same as that "feminine principle" advocated by some; my conclusion is that they have much in common, but that it is safer to focus on the trinity because there is less dualism in the idea.

OTHER THREES AND FOURS

I have so far described my natural four-fold analysis, and then my realization that there is an alternative three-fold scheme. To what extent is there already a strong three-fold tradition that I am simply not tuned in to? What is the point of this campaigning effort if the majority of my readers have been thinking in threes all their lives?

Looking for other three-fold schemes I began with the symbolic system of astrology. Here we have a fourfold scheme very much on the lines that I have described: it is of the four elements Earth, Air, Fire and Water. And there is a two-fold scheme within it of positive and negative or masculine and feminine signs (where Fire and Air are positive and Earth and Water are negative). But we also have an equally important three-fold scheme of Cardinal, Fixed and Mutable signs.

That would apparently put three-fold thinking clearly on the map as an equal partner to fourfold analysis and the masculine/feminine dualism, but is that how we see it in practice? Not at all: popular astrology borrows heavily from the four elements - every introductory magazine article will tell you how well Water and Earth signs get on with each other and how hard it is for Air and Water - but how often do we see the triplicity of Cardinal, Fixed and Mutable being described?

Cardinal signs initiate action, set things in motion and stir things up. Fixed signs hold onto what is and keep it going; they do not "start", they "maintain". Mutable signs see the ending of projects and the hope of new beginnings; they are the catalysts of change who will introduce a new level that spells the death of the old and its transmutation to a new plane, ready to be set into motion again by the Cardinal type. Now, if you are heavily into the four elements it is less easy to grasp these three types and, as with the Triple Goddess, there is a temptation to interpret them in the terms already understood. Isn't the Cardinal type a bit like Fire, the Fixed like Earth and the mutable like Water? Am I right? Of course not. Because, as astrology itself shows, all four elements exist in Cardinal, Fixed and Mutable forms. The three-fold scheme has to be independent of the two or four-fold schemes, not just a simplification of it.

In Appendix B I include a trinitarian ritual I devised and performed: in it the congregation was divided into three roles based on whether they were predominately Cardinal, Fixed or Mutable. Many rituals and self discovery workshops at some point divide the room into four segments and suggest that those present sit in those areas and play certain roles - dividing us into Earth, Air, Fire and Water types is a typical example. But how many rituals and workshops use a three-fold frame for their exploration? I suspect very few. Four-fold analysis and two-fold dialogue where you "confront" aspects of your inner self are the main tools of self discovery and magic. Later in this book I will be suggesting that the trinity could become a useful addition to the toolkit for both self discovery and magic.

Notice how the astrological trinity had a sense of time or flux in it, and how that contrasted with the more categorical analysis of the quaternity. Cardinal begins, Fixed continues and Mutable ends to allow rebirth and new beginnings. Whereas Earth, Air, Fire and Water are distinct categories that encourage us to typecast each other. As with the three-fold Goddess, it is the trinity that gives a sense of flow or organic growth through cycles, while the four-fold scheme tends to crystallise out into rigid types.

Another example comes from alchemy. Alchemy is a very difficult and impenetrable subject to the modern mind. Ask a hundred sympathetic people about it and most would recall its dualistic aim - to transform lead into gold - and a sizeable majority might recognise in alchemy the origin of the four-fold classification of the elements. But few would be able to expound on the other great scheme, the trinity of Sulphur, Salt and Mercury. I cannot say much about that trinity myself, I never found it as clear as the four elements, but it seems to line up with the astrological trinity quite well: Sulphur being an aggressive initiator, Salt the solid sustainer, and Mercury the communicator and transformer - with the same suggestion of an overall process that carries through a cycle.

That cyclical flow is most obvious in another trinity, that of the mantra AUM which is analysed into beginning, middle and ending. There is a strong tradition that the ending or death in the "m" sound is just the transition to a new birth or incarnation, and the upward spiral of this cycle was emphasised by Aleister Crowley when he derived the alternative version AUMGN where the sound returns at another level as a "GN" nasal buzz.

Less obvious is the sense of flow or time in another great trinity - that of the christian God. When I discussed my ideas with someone who knew much more about christian history than myself they pointed out something which could strongly support my thesis if it turns out to be historically correct. Apparently our strong identification of the cross as the prime symbol of christianity has not always been so clear. In the earliest days the symbol of the trinity did the vital job of explaining Christ's role as being a manifestation of the one God and so keeping out any criticism that they had taken the one God of the Jews and created a dualism of father and son from it. In those earliest times the calvary cross as symbol was much less in evidence, in fact the more obvious use of the cross was the equal armed one contained in the early Chi Rho symbol. But a few centuries later the cross of Calvary began to predominate as the christian symbol, and this seems to have some parallelism with christianity becoming more aggressive as it took over and repressed the military Mithraic tradition. The trinity went under, the cross was raised, and christianity went to war. I do hope this is true - it supports my thesis so well - pity 'bout all the folks what got killed in the process, innit? And is it too fanciful to see in the unequal form of the Calvary cross, with its one longer leg and three short ones, some echo of the trinity that it swallowed up?

These explorations suggest to me that there is a tradition of trinitarian thinking, but it is far from being widely practiced. Even in popular examples like astrology, the three is largely overlooked in favour of the two and the four. Three-fold schemes exist and have a great history, but they seem to be dormant or denied in our thinking which is so strongly inclined to analyse into twos and fours. Maybe something very important has been excluded?

So my main argument is this: there are ways of thought which could save us from the divisiveness inherent in dualistic thinking. Three-fold thinking in particular will be seen to have a flowing, organic quality which is a vital addition to the separating effects of dualism and the crystallising quality that can make four-fold analysis become too rigid. These ways of thought already exist but must be rediscovered, re-explored and re-affirmed, but we will need to be on guard that in so doing we do not simply slip back into dualism or re-interpret the trinity on dualistic lines so that it fails to provide any solution and falls back into disuse.

PARS
DUO

ooooo

DE RE
IGNIS

The river which flows from the South is a river of Fire. Some may fear to be consumed in its brilliance but, for my salamander soul, it is a haven from the waters of the West. Here I may rest and spread my bedraggled feathers in the heat until ready to rise Phoenix-like in the East.

Alas, my son, for good intentions. I set out to seek that balm which could sooth our wounded world and prepare for you a wholesome future with Hope's rosy fingers touching the Eastern horizon and drawing aside the veils of Night. Plunging into the waters of the West I found opposition and discord snapping at my limbs. Even Adam, bathing in the purer waters of the source, could not help but stir sleeping dualities from the depths. So should I now take up the sword and banish duality by force? To what avail? for the very sword is itself duality by nature - a two edged weapon which will return upon its wielder.

There is another technique of separation, however, and that is separation by Fire. Like alchemists of old we can apply a gentle heat to drive out water and part the elements. Thus we do not avoid division, but rather contain it within our alembic so that nothing is lost, nothing is ignored.

Fire brings heat and fire brings light. Let us shine the rays of our torch into those depths and garner knowledge and understanding of their perils. Who knows, the enemy we once sought to eradicate may thus be revealed and, being revealed, may turn out to have a face of friendship too?

For how can we learn to think in threes if we have not yet learnt to think truly and wisely in ones and twos?

THINKING IN ONES

You cannot really think in ones. Try it.

First affirm that you can think. Choose a comfortable meditative posture and start with a dualistic idea: for example "the universe is a battle between the forces of Good and the forces of Evil", or "matter is a dance of positive and negative charges", or "politics is a juggling act between the individual and the state"... Given any such dualism the mind is as happy as a child in a sandpit, it can play with it for hours.

Having done that, now try instead to contemplate a single, monistic idea: for example "infinite, boundless space", or "the universe as pure Love", or "all phenomena are pure chance". Given a single thing to contemplate, the mind is almost at once bored. It runs looking for the edges. Contemplate eternity, and the mind wants to know when it began. Insist that everything is pure chance and the mind will dig for possible exceptions or will seek a meaning behind chance.

So "thinking in ones" is not quite the right phrase: we do not really think in ones, what we do with ones is assume them. Assumption is a static state, and it does not attract attention like thought, so that is why it is easy to overlook. The problems which we met in the last section all seemed to be dualistic, and that fact might tempt us to turn attention to eliminating duality in order to provide a solution. But I suspect that we would have failed because even deeper assumptions lie like sediment beneath those depths. We could dynamite every duality out of those waters and still end up trapped in the mud. What little chance, for example, of eliminating or even transcending duality if one is living in the unconscious assumption that duality is the basis of all manifestation?

Thinking in ones is a matter of unconscious belief, or unconscious assumptions. By their nature such beliefs are unremarkable, for if we remark them they must be conscious ideas and, as our attempt to think in ones showed, you cannot be really conscious of one thing without an awareness of possible alternatives. This means that it is very difficult to discuss thinking in ones because the process is by nature invisible. So, rather than attempt to do it on something as complex as an individual, let me begin by taking an easier route and looking at ideas in our society.

I start with popular scientific notions. Long ago most Europeans assumed that the Bible's account of the world was substantially correct: a world made by God in seven days or at least in seven symbolic stages, Man and Woman created to have dominion over the world but with an inherent imperfection which lead to corruption and the need for divine intervention to save mankind in preparation for a second coming... or something along those lines.

Then around the sixteenth century a different idea began slowly to spread: an idea of an automatic, mechanistic world where matter not God was the absolute. It is ironic to consider that this idea, which we now imagine to be the absolute antithesis of magic, would in its early stages have invoked accusations of witchcraft and dabbling with the devil. John Dee, famous as Queen Elizabeth's astrologer, never lived down his reputation for having dealings with the devil - a reputation based largely on the mechanical "special effects" he created for the theatre as a student. Indeed, an idea that now seems so commonplace as to be positively pernicious, then seemed like the wildest speculation of a demonically obsessed mind. So used are we now to the materialistic world view, even if we prefer to oppose it, that it takes an effort of imagination to see how outrageous and "magical" it would have seemed in those days. If you had been brought up with the idea of an intelligent creator - and there is nothing inherently "illogical" about such an idea - then the suggestion that the chance movements of dumb matter could have organised themselves into intelligent life would indeed seem like hocus pocus.

What began as wild speculation slowly began to be affirmed by centuries of scientific experiment. Thus the idea slowly took over and ousted the biblical version of truth until, by the end of the nineteenth century, everyone was paying lip service to the idea of a mechanical world of solid atoms, a world in which you would only need absolute knowledge of its laws and absolute computational ability to be able to predict every single outcome of every event for ever more. Christianity still survived, but not for its description of the universe so much as for its moral and social values.

Then, into that rock solid world of utter certainty, there came a new generation of apparently wild speculations which suggested that matter was not so absolute and certain after all. Relativity and quantum mechanics - what we now label "the new physics" - first began to blossom in the opening years of this century and it is interesting to plot the spread of this new creed.

As before, ideas which the establishment now takes for granted began as outlaws beyond the pale in the deterministic establishment of nineteenth century science. Relativity and quantum mechanics would have been unheard of outside very select circles for the first decade or two. And they probably only made their name on

account of the opposition they met from the establishment. Having been brought to wider scientific notice,
however, word began to leak out to the general public,
mostly in the form of "gee whiz, the things these crazy
scientists think of" articles which bordered on science fic-
tion. So you find occasional headlines in pre-war magazines which announce a new potential source of unlimit-
ed energy - or else the end of the universe - if the atom
was ever to be split and set off the predicted "chain reaction".

Of course, the "man in the street" never really
believed any of this in his heart until 1945 when the first
atom bomb was dropped. Then suddenly he was obliged
to believe it because it had now been revealed as practical
fact. So during the fifties and sixties nobody would laugh
at Einstein any more, because he was now a "genius" and
must therefore be right. The world must really be an
insubstantial tissue of fleeting particles because it had
been "proved". But hardly anyone actually believed this
truth in their hearts - they all went on living as if matter
was all that mattered, more so than ever indeed.

By the sixties these "new" ideas were being taught
in schools and a new generation was being brought up
where "the new physics" was not a revolutionary idea you
discovered outside the classroom, but rather the establishment creed, the accepted truth.

As I write this it is the nineteen nineties and most
of the population is still behaving as if they believed the
world to be a solid mechanical place which follows rigid,
discoverable laws; but there is also a new feeling, typified
by the New Age movement, which suggests that some

people really are beginning to believe in their hearts and bodies that the world could be a curious manifestation of quantum and relativistic events. Be careful: I am not suggesting that people now have a sophisticated understanding of particle physics, but simply that the feeling that "everything is solid and obeys fixed laws" is being replaced with a general feeling that "nothing is solid and things are only predictable on average". The new physics is not only being paid lip service in our heads, it is beginning to be practiced in our hearts.

But the process is by no means complete. The real triumph of the new physics will be when nobody bothers to talk about it any more - except when conjured up as defence against the latest silly new ideas.

What this long winded account was meant to show has nothing to do with physics, but rather the way an idea, world-view or theory seems to enter, infest and finally establish itself in the public mind. In particular I want to show the difference between conscious acceptance when "we know it must be true because it has been proved", and unconscious acceptance when we instinctively know and live the idea because it is taken for granted.

Often these two levels of belief are at odds. In the above example, the "proof" of the New Physics at Hiroshima did not mark the end of materialism as a way of life, but rather its establishment in triumph: the fifties saw a surge of appreciation of solid matter all round the world, and material goods, rather than psychological, social or spiritual well-being, was established as the measure for quality of life. Similarly I suspect that the Church was never before so powerful as it became in the nine-teenth century. However much it ruled humanity's conscious beliefs in earlier centuries, it was still struggling for their hearts and bodies in the face of protestantism and endless heresies within its own ranks - many pagan traditions and celebrations survived centuries of persecution in Britain only to fizzle out in the Victorian era. At the time when christianity was losing its control over our thinking it was the discredited Bible that began to rule society, it was the Church that finally took its place as a power behind the secular establishment. Even in communism's out-and-out rebellion against spiritual tradition we see a re-affirmation of christian principles of compassion for the underdog and sharing with one's fellow men.

This is what I mean by thinking in ones: as long as an idea is just one of a set of alternatives, then it is still being tossed about in the ball-game of consciousness. But once it has taken root as Accepted Truth, then it can rule our lives as an inner tyrant. The strength of such an idea lies in its utter unquestioning acceptance. In return for such acceptance we are blessed with a sense of security and there is peace in the land.

This is the formula for the ideal state of harmony as described in the Tao Teh Ching.

"In days of old those who successfully practiced Tao did not use it to enlighten the people but rather to make them ignorant. The more knowledge people have, the harder they are to rule." And "given a small country he could create a culture where even if there were devices which would reduce labour ten or a hundred times nobody would bother to use them... there might be boats

and carriages but no-one would go about in them... people would have no use for writing... be content with their food, clothing and homes... The next country might be within earshot but his people would grow old and die happily without ever going there".

There is a blissful innocence and contentment in one-fold thought, but it is the bliss of ignorance depending on no other belief being considered and the one belief itself being so taken for granted as to be almost unknown. It is a Garden of Eden state which is only vulnerable because of the serpent that encourages us to take of the Tree of Knowledge. What then happens is that we become aware of the one belief and begin to question it.

In this stable dictatorship the ultimate ruler is concealed behind a hierarchy of minor tyrants. Above I described how in Victorian times everyone was talking about mechanistic, humanistic ideas while acting out the beliefs of the Church. Now we talk about the New Physics while still acting out the principles of a mechanistic world view - assuming, for example, that everything which happens must have a cause which we can trace. But behind all three world views - traditional Christianity, Mechanistic Materialism and New Physics - there is the assumption that there is One Truth towards which we are ever progressing. We may hear complaints that British workmanship or children's manners are not what they used to be, but no-one ever suggests that truth might not be as good as it used to be. Perhaps truth itself is subject to change: maybe matter really was solid before this century, and perhaps it took so long to split the first atom because the local universe had first to re-structure itself seamlessly in order to allow that to happen?

Religions seem to evolve towards monotheism. To start with every rock or tree has its own god, then these become organised into hierarchies until we end up with just one god, even if he is allowed a bureaucracy of angels to help him rule the universe. Unfortunately for religious leaders this movement towards unity does not cease: having reduced all gods to one God it is still too much to have matter distinct from God, thus matter becomes God and monotheism evolves into materialism. (This is actually the triumph of the Goddess - she began her life representing matter, she loses her throne to a male God of the spiritual realm, and she ends up deposing that God and becoming the only reality. Matter as "mater" or "mother" becomes the one truth in a materialist culture.) However, the move towards monotheism continues and it cannot tolerate the distinction between an objective material world and our own subjective experience of it. So the New Physics in turn deposes matter, and we will soon be left with one truth - a universe of information as the ultimate monotheism.

All this demonstrates the power of one-fold thinking. Monotheism triumphs over polytheism because it has such inner strength and security, it in turn gives way to science simply because science is even more profound-ly monotheistic. At each stage we become more effective because we are operating from an even more solid base. Science is like the perfect tyrant of the Tao Teh Ching: it keeps our bellies full and keeps us amused, it even allows us to question its findings, but that in turn makes it very hard for society to question the scientific process itself.

Pause.

I'm getting a bit fed up with society as an example. I chose it because it is easier to start with. Writers can waffle on for pages saying things like "tossed about by the winds of fashion we drift from craze to craze blah blah blah" and the reader thinks "uhu... uhu... yes ..." because the fact that "we" includes me and you is forgotten in the general picture of humanity as a sort of amorphous blob being tossed about. If instead I had written "you, John Smith of 14 Trellis Mews, Milton Keynes are tossed about by the winds of fashion" the reader might well protest that there was a definite moment at 3.30pm that day when they distinctly recalled resisting the winds of fashion.

So let us look at the individual. I propose that we all have some sort of hierarchy of assumptions or inner tyrants within our unconscious minds. I propose that this is basically a good and necessary thing, because a firm assumption is an excellent basis for decisive and effective action and it makes for peace in one's inner kingdom; but I also propose that greater wisdom comes from being aware of these assumptions and knowing how they make us act.

The problem is that it is not easy to uncover these assumptions simply because they are most effective when left alone. Dismiss Christianity from your conscious beliefs, and its deeply ingrained principles are left free in the unconscious to pull the strings of your behaviour. Accept that materialism is "not true" and you have pushed it off the throne and into the executive office. So it is always easier to see unconscious beliefs in other people.

We shall see later that we really need duality to become conscious so, although talking about one-fold belief, I have actually introduced a little duality in order to make the discussion possible. For example: I suggested a dualistic split between our conscious and our unconscious beliefs. So let us take advantage of this split when first looking at other people's inner tyrants.

Have you noticed how some people over-affirm certain things, to the extent that you begin to wonder if the opposite might not be true? It is ok, for example, to admit a fondness for traditional values, but what if the speaker goes on and on about them at every opportunity? Surely a central tenet of traditional values is that the Good must triumph. So, assuming traditional values themselves to be good, there is less rather than more need to champion them because they will triumph anyway. Thus we sense that the person who defends traditional values overmuch must actually have too little faith in them, seeing them as a feeble force being swept away by greater powers and therefore desperately needing to be defended.

Similarly, the person who goes on and on about the need for "taking a tough line": the very fact that there is such an urge to support the tough line suggests an inner belief that the tough line is actually a weak thing which is everywhere being swamped by an overpowering tide of wishy washy wetness. Again, the person who takes an exaggerated line in defending Nature against the incursion of Mankind does seem to be affirming that Nature is

now an unnatural thing which requires human intervention to keep it working.

What we are doing in these examples is using the
scalpel of dualism to uncover other people's inner truths.
Having done that for a bit you might be able to try it on
yourself and uncover a few of your own inner tyrants. But
unfortunately the method depends upon dualistic battles
to attract attention to the tyrant. When these battles are
in full cry it isn't easy to observe oneself dispassionately,
and when the battles do not take place there is nothing to
go on. So I suggest a three-fold rather than a two-fold
approach.

You could, for example, divide a large sheet of
paper into three columns and head them: "What I would
like to believe", "What I am supposed to believe" and
"What I really believe". Then down the left hand side you
could put a range of topics such as "Myself", "God",
"Magic" and so on. Thinking of myself, for example, I
would like to believe that I am a special person with an
important role to play in this world, and that I am seeking to discover what that role is. However I suspect that I
am supposed to believe that we are all created equal but
that our environment shapes us for different roles.
Recognising the difference between those two beliefs
somehow serves as a springboard which helps me to
uncover a deep belief that I am in fact innately inferior to
other people and am seeking some magical activity or
remedy in order to make up for that fact.

Many years ago I hit upon this formula as a way
of exploring my attitude to magic. I realised how I wanted to believe that there was something called "magic" that

would open up doorways to mystery and blow open the dogmatic materialistic world-view, whereas I was supposed to believe that the materialistic world-view was true. Jumping from there I realised that not only did I believe that materialistic view was the truth but I also needed the security it gave me. The result was that I would attempt to perform magic and would bungle it in order to confirm that it did not exist. My conscious hunt for magic was actually an unconscious field sport that ended in the death of the hunted.

I will now divert slightly to explain what I did with that knowledge of a split between my conscious desire to believe in magic and my emotional need to confirm a rock solid universe. My next step was to examine my ingrained materialism and compare it item by item with what I was "supposed to believe". Yes, I did believe in cause and effect; I did believe that chance could eventually throw up complex living organisms; I did believe that the motions of matter could even generate intelligence and conscious self-awareness... After a lot of exploration and peeling away all sorts of magical ideas that I wished to believe in, I eventually came to a level where my inner belief did not exactly match popular materialistic dogma: I really felt that the world was more connected up than reductionism and atomistic philosophy would allow. That each and every particle in the universe was an independent entity with no more than outside forces linking it to other particles I could not accept, because it seemed to imply a squandering of information which went against the economy that I had been taught to look for in all phenomena. From that discovery grew my subsequent magical world-view.

Let me attempt a picture to explain why this was so important to me. If I describe popular materialistic dogma as a sort of concrete desert you might get the picture. Not liking that desert I had been trying consciously to banish it by painting it, covering it with plastic flowers and the occasional real potted palm. In other words I had been looking for superficial magics to cover up the concrete desert. Now I was clearing away all that stuff, getting back to bare concrete. In doing so, however, I eventually uncovered a crack in the concrete and through that crack a few neglected wisps of living grass were poking. Having discovered these I could cultivate them: plants began to push through the cracks and force up the concrete. A sense of real magic was growing and I could now look back and see how my earlier efforts had actually hindered this from happening by choking the only real growth. What is more, I could see how many other people were crying out for magic yet chasing it in a similar way which simply re-affirmed its non-existence.

This diversion has allowed me to give value to the exercise of uncovering hidden tyrants: it shows how their negative effects can be reduced. Once it is recognised, you can either negotiate with an inner tyrant, or else elect a better idea to its throne. Beware, however, of the fallacy of democracy which is to believe that just because you elect someone to power that person will remain on your side. The object is to elect a new tyrant whose self-interest is in greater harmony with your own self interest.

You see, I consider that, among all the petty tyrants in our brains, there lies one very deep and very very powerful tyrant which is the Principle of Unity about which I am writing here. Concealing that tyrant is another of nearly equal power, and that is the Principle of Duality. The combined power of those two tyrants has convinced us that there is but One Thing behind all manifestation, and that One Thing is the Principle of Duality. Thus the Principle of Trinity - and who knows what other principles yet to be explored - has been forced out of power. This book is a manifesto for the recovery and reinstating of the principle of trinity in our lives.

THINKING IN TWOS

I have already introduced thinking in twos: in the last section I suggested that you meditate on some dualistic notion such as life being a battle between good and evil forces.

Unity was described as a lovely secure state, typified by those Tao Teh Ching quotations which suggested that the perfect ruler was a sort of invisible power that simply maintained a state of ignorant contentment. I pointed it that this was the very real bliss of ignorance and it was a paradise which was vulnerable to serpentine prompting to eat of the Tree of Knowledge.

When the masses in that ideal taoist state become too clever, they want to know what is going on, and whether things might not be even better for a few changes. Similarly, when consciousness is born from the unconscious, it begins to ask questions. So what now must the wise ruler do?

If we ask recent wise rulers - Hitler, Thatcher, Saddam Hussein and umpteen others - they all know the answer: *create an enemy*. Once consciousness has made the first split in your unity, the best thing to do is to tear it wide open by introducing the duality of "us and them".

The effect is wonderful. An enormous amount of energy is released by this splitting of the atom of unity. Your kingdom, which was seeming to lose its unity and evolve into a simmering cauldron of dissent, now seems to discover a new and brilliant level of unity: suddenly everyone is wearing the same uniform, marching in step and speaking the same slogans. That old state of harmony seems in comparison to have been an aimless pool of diverse, bumbling citizens going their separate ways.

This is the great illusion of duality: it is manifest so vividly that the effect is of a unity more unified than unity itself. Coming from unity, we have an instinct to adopt just one side of the duality and reject the other side by denying it in ourselves - the result is an electrifying and yet strangely fragile illusion of unity. Rather like the glass rod stroked with a piece of silk by the physics teacher, all the negative charges are driven off to produce a highly charged state which can be released with one explosive spark.

As an example of such a war consider capitalism and communism. As far as I know there would be few Victorians who felt incensed about this issue: communism might be seen as a primitive christian state and capitalism, although a departure from that, could always redeem itself by its good works for the poor and needy. It was Marx and his followers who are reputed to have defined the battle between these two states: communism was set up as a champion against capitalism.

Now I do not want to read too much into this example, but I cannot help feeling that Marxist opposition to capitalism served to give it life. True, there was plenty of capitalism in the nineteenth century, but it seems to have been in the background. There were dynamic individuals amassing great amounts of capital, but they are remembered more for their products. We might hear of a "shipping magnate" of a "diamond merchant" or "wool trader" among the newly rich, and the emphasis is on a great deal of industrial activity which just happens to create great wealth. Only when under attack from communism did capitalism get a strong sense of itself, an illusion of unity which presented capitalism as a thing in itself rather than as a mechanism to serve other purposes. The twentieth century's rich are known more as capitalists than for their industrial base - who knows what actual commodity it was that Paul Getty produced to earn his fortunes?

The end point of this split was that two great nations were at cold war and divided the whole world in the process. And I could not but delight in the irony of it because the greatest extremes of this battle were so nearly identical. The true American redneck, with all his dogmatism and outraged sense of justice, need only be stripped of his jeans and check shirt and stuck into an overcoat and fur hat to become the archetypal Soviet commissar. The real ideological gulf lay between the redneck and his liberal compatriots and yet, when faced with the Soviet threat, the redneck would feel at one with the liberal and even describe his stance as "liberal opposition to Soviet totalitarianism".

Duality produces immense clarity. Its symbol is the sword or knife of analysis, and everything is thereby divided by it into clear black and white. Yet you need only step out of it to see it as an illusion or game. As with my static electricity analogy, the greatest power of duality, and the greatest fragility, comes when the two opposing charges are brought as close as possible. The immense energy of the redneck's attack on communism is not in spite of his temperamental closeness to the communist, but because of it. The rigidly ordered Soviet lifestyle with its lack of dissent and low crime is just what would best suit the redneck, and yet it represents everything he despises. I suspect that Nazism would never have been so rabidly anti-semitic but for the suspicion of Jewish blood in Hitler's ancestry. The fundamentalist christian who raves against the forces of Satan and insists that thousands of babies are being sacrificed every year in Satan's name even though the police find no trace of such crimes, that christian clearly has a monstrous inner evil to cope with: is it the guilt of millions of Jews and Moslems who were slaughtered in Christ's name? or the umpteen million turkeys sacrificed every Christmas? or the slaughter in Northern Ireland? or the thousands of victims of pederastic priests? Whatever haunts the christian fanatic is projected manyfold onto his imagined enemies, and if you are not totally with him you are most certainly on the side of Satan. Thus Satan gains power through opposition - only through christian efforts are we persuaded that he even exists - and becomes more interesting than those who oppose him.

Duality is so utterly real when you are in the game - nothing could be more clear cut and urgent - and yet it is such an illusion when you step out of it and observe its dynamics. Good / evil, black / white, rich / poor, man / nature, right / left, revolution / reaction, christian / pagan, liberal / totalitarian... whatever name the game has it is all basically the one game of "God versus Devil" played out on a black and white board of fractal complexity.

When I was writing about thinking in ones I made some effort to point out the benefits - the sense of peace, security and harmony - as well as the drawbacks because I did not want to banish unity so much as recognise it and put it in its place. So also with duality. Although its divisiveness can lead ultimately to a desperate sense of paranoia and war, it should be acknowledged as a wonderful source of excitement and energy. If we could only play it as a game instead of becoming caught in its illusion then what a joy duality could be. Instead it turns sour and we yearn for primal unity - whereas we should, I believe, be looking forward to the trinity.

In Appendix C I include an essay in praise of devil worship which takes up the positive aspects of duality. It obviously lies outside the main theme of this book, but it fits with my suggestion that our approach to the trinity should not be via denying or deposing unity and duality, but rather by putting them back where they belong in the scheme of things.

As to exploring the power of duality in our selves, the principle has already been suggested in the last section where I introduced a duality of conscious versus unconscious components of the mind. Whenever the outward manner of someone seems to show an extreme face, we look for the polar quality to be hidden within in equally extreme form - like an equal and opposite reaction. So the christian anti-satanic campaigner is giving voice to a correspondingly powerful inner Satan, and the rabid revolutionary is exercising a tyrannical desire to impose his own will upon society.

But the division does not have to lie across the conscious / unconscious threshold. You can have the office tyrant who goes home to submit to a domineering wife, the spiritual leader who amasses immense wealth by preaching denial of worldly goods, the paedophile who expresses his love as abuse or the anti-abuse campaigner who torments children psychologically in order to extract stories of physical abuse...

A particularly interesting and helpful example could be to study the dynamics between a victim and those who bully him. It has become immensely unfashionable to suggest that a rape victim could have been asking for it, and it must indeed be very offensive for such a victim to be told that this could be the case. But, in view of the general bully/victim dynamic, it is a very natural question to raise and even in very clear cut cases of abuse it would be as well for the matter to be considered at some point - the main difficulty being to know at what point it could be tactfully and helpfully raised without merely adding a new angle to the victimisation.

Myself I am more of a victim-type than a bully, yet I can recall my schooldays when certain individuals seemed to exude a whiny and intoxicating wetness that invoked a huge urge to thump them or torment them with words. In sado-masochistic circles it is apparently the masochists who set the agenda. My own experience of being the soft one who goes along with other people's wishes is that you develop a marvellous survival strength which is denied to the bully who gets his way. After a while you notice that the bully insists on getting his way because he is inwardly too weak to survive anything else (or so he unconsciously believes) while the victim goes along with it because he is now tough enough to survive whatever the world chucks at him. The schoolmasterly cliche "this hurts me more than it will hurt you" takes on new significance and a whole tangle of paradoxes suggest themselves: not only could it have been the suggestion of Jewish blood that fired Hitler's anti-semitism, it could also be that the final result of his holocaust was to compel the world to restore to the Jews their promised land as compensation.

In this way we can explore the bully/victim dynamic in ourselves and discover maybe a tendency to impose our will on certain situations by invoking guilt in others, while in other situations we take control and feel vaguely bad about it. This leads to a general search for other dualities to see how they rule our lives: there are a whole range of sub-personalities based upon dualistic pairs such as child/adult, freedom/dependence, mystic/pragmatist, work/play, change/maintenance, love/will and so on. Wherever you feel inclined to identify strongly with one pole of such a pair, look again for signs that the opposite pole is also active in your nature. The value of this exercise is that you can learn to transcend those dualities which are tearing you apart.

Imagine, for example, the eternal child who is deliciously irresponsible and who is forever asking others to take charge and manage his affairs. Is this a problem? Not if he finds a manager and settles to a comfortable relationship with that person. But if, more typically, anyone who has the necessary stability is rebelled against and jeered at until they give up in despair, then there is a recurring problem and the child could well discover that it has been giving the orders, that it has its own inner authority so strong that it not only keeps the child from growing up but also challenges anyone else who might exercise authority over the child. If the individual can recognise both sides of the polarity inside himself rather than pushing one out on others, then there is a possibility for inner dialogue. The inner authority can work with the inner child to produce a less unbalanced nature.

The dynamic between authority and childishness is a lot of fun and a great source of colour in our lives. If it sometimes overcomes us and polarises us into a state of war with ourselves and other people, then the blame lies not so much with duality as with our lack of alternatives to duality.

THE ONE AND THE TWO

Having been introduced to unity and duality there is a temptation to compare them and weigh them up. Which is more fundamental? Which is more wholesome? Which is more productive? Which brings greater happiness?

Be careful. Contrasting unity with duality is a dualistic activity based on the pair of "opposites" unity/duality, and for that very reason it is hard not to take sides.

One example is to equate unity with God. Then duality "must" be of the Devil, and suddenly we see his two horns symbolising this "truth". Yes, it is the devil who seeks to divide the divine unity, to set us against each other. Is not the illusion of duality I referred to just the illusion of all the Devil's work: the maya of the material universe? Duality is seen as the basis of all manifest existence and so becomes the original sin against God's unity. Did I not suggest that the fall which cast us out of Paradise was because we were tempted by the serpent to eat of the Tree of Knowledge? Has not the division of the sexes lead to endless problems?

Very soon we become incensed about this wicked state of duality. We become crusaders intent on stamping out duality in all its forms. There is but one desire, to get back to that divine innocence of unity, to become one with God once more.

The trouble with this crusade is that it is no more an attack on duality than it is an expression of the very duality referred to: that of unity versus duality. It is, as it were, the Devil tricking us into doing his work in the name of God.

Another example has already been referred to in the first part: it is to equate unity with the feminine and duality with the masculine on the basis that the manifestation of unity is peaceful and supportive while the manifestation of duality is dynamic and divisive. Then the belief that our society is dominated by the masculine influence of the patriarchy leads to a desire to champion the feminine virtues of unity over the masculinity of duality. This too is a dangerous game, and a paradoxical one because there is an equal tradition that the number one, like all odd numbers, is masculine and solar, while the number two, like all even numbers, is feminine and lunar. In this tradition unity is seen as rigid and dogmatic, knowing no alternatives, while duality is typified by the two horns of the moon and the ebb and flow between opposites. Whichever way we take our symbols, the crusade for unity again becomes the by-product of a duality - this time it is the battle of the sexes.

We have studied unity and we have studied duality. If we stop at this point we live in a dualistic world with only two alternatives - unity or duality - and it is almost inevitable that we will take sides sooner or later. It is too late to eliminate duality, that innocence is already lost, so we must move on to other systems in order to populate our universe with more ideas. As soon as there is another number available we need no longer be trapped in a dualistic world because there are further choices.

THINKING IN FOURS

In the first part we saw the meeting between two dualities. The first was of men who liked big tits versus those who did not. The second was of men who liked women with legs versus those who did not. And we saw how the two dualities merged into a fourfold analysis of types.

There could have been other outcomes. My difference of opinion with mine host could have divided our party into those who felt tits were the basic key while those who insisted that legs were the fundamental criterion of male choice and we could have ended up fighting about a tits/legs duality.

Or my duality could have been swallowed up by mine host's as he argued *"your idea about legs sounds very clever, but can't you see what it tells us about you? How on earth could you fail to notice something as obvious as a woman's breasts? It can only mean that you are deeply inhibited and probably had a very unsatisfactory relationship with your mother. Yes, Daughters with negligible breasts do tend to have long legs and you have obviously latched onto that but are putting up this "Amazon" smokescreen to hide the fact that you suffer deep, unconscious guilt about your attraction to the immature woman. You, my friend have simply illustrated my point by being so obviously attracted to the daughter type even though you refuse to acknowledge the fact. And you should really see an analyst about that Mother problem."*

Or conversely the host's duality could have been swallowed by mine as I argued *"it's got nothing to do with Mothers and Daughters. The problem goes back to the moment of conception itself because it is all about the dualism of flesh and spirit. The man who loves the Amazon is loving a strong woman of the world, a creature of flesh and action. While the man who pursues the Witch or Priestess is seeking to transcend flesh via the spirit. Whether it is strong legs or big breasts makes little difference, the desire is to drown oneself in earthly woman flesh and that sets one apart from those who seek the negation of these qualities in the slender innocence of youth or the transcendent mystery of the spirit. You who are trapped in the battle between flesh and spirit are attempting to make light of the matter by representing this dilemma in trivial theories about Mothers and Daughters.*"

Instead of any of these three bellicose possibilities something else happened: our dualities married to become a four-fold analysis and peace was restored.

Four-fold thinking is far less combative than two-fold thinking. Whereas the nature of duality is to bring division, dynamism and discord, four seems to bring thoughtfulness, analysis and a sort of security.

I suggested that we try to meditate in twos and in ones, and we found that the mind could think about dualities very easily. So there is a strong element of thoughtfulness in the number two, yet we are always drawn to taking sides in order to achieve that false sense of unity that I described. Faced with a set of four possibilities there is far less desire to champion one of them against the other: instead we want to study their relationship and their interaction.

Typically the relationship is of two pairs of opposites presented as the arms of a cross. Using that early example: the words on the cross could be Mother versus Daughter and Amazon versus Witch. Other examples are Earth, Air, Fire and Water; Sensation, Intuition, Thinking and Feeling; Tough, Tender, Radical and Conservative; Hot or Cold, Moist or Dry; North, South, East and West... and so on as shown in Figure 1 opposite.

Although the nature of such analysis is non-combative, the two-dimensional representation of it does suggest two pairs of opposites and so fourfold thinking can

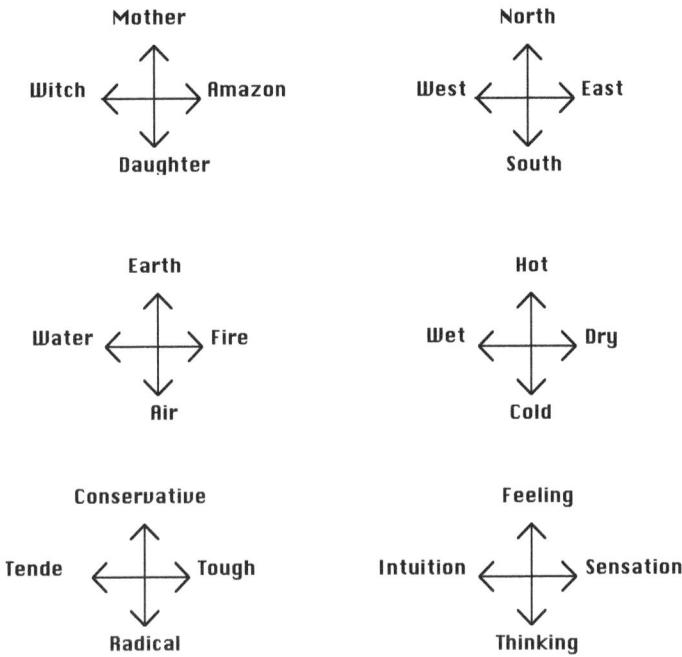

Mother

Witch ←—↑—→ Amazon

Daughter

North

West ←—↑—→ East

South

Earth

Water ←—↑—→ Fire

Air

Hot

Wet ←—↑—→ Dry

Cold

Conservative

Tende ←—↑—→ Tough

Radical

Feeling

Intuition ←—↑—→ Sensation

Thinking

Figure 1.

Examples of four-fold analyses. (Note that these are independent
examples to be considered separately, not cross-referred.)

retain that sense of dualism and it can break down into
warring opposites under some circumstances.

However, four-fold analysis more often meets
opposition from people who say things like "I hate these
over-simple models", or "why do you have to stick labels
onto everything?". In the first part I suggested that,
although I had set out to provide a compass to chart our
course upon an exciting ocean exploration, many readers
would see my effort as no more than a tedious typecasting exercise.

Both two-fold and four-fold thinking can lead to forms of stagnation. In the first case it is a tense stagnation typified by the cold war of two enemies too heavily armed to dare launch an attack. In the second case it is more like a freezing out. Once one has classified one's friends into Earth, Air, Fire and Water types - although an interesting and informative exercise in its own right - the tendency is to leave the analysis in a "so what?" state. Everyone is now neatly labelled and there is nothing more to do. This is what can be so offensive about typecasting, once a woman has been labelled as, say, an Amazon type she can have difficulty shaking the
label: if she decides to become a Mother it will be seen as just her latest Amazon "project"; if she takes up Witchery it will be seen as a bid to further extend her power; if she expresses the Daughter nature she will be praised for her strapping Amazonian youthfulness.

So I can understand why people are not universally enamoured of four-fold analysis: it does indeed seem to lead towards a sterile understanding. But mine own hunch is that the real problem is more fundamental: it is that in progressing from two-fold to four-fold thinking we have skipped the number three and so deprived the soul of a certain sustenance it needs.

Time, therefore, to look properly at threefold thinking.

THINKING IN THREES

This is a little more difficult. When I described thinking in ones and twos I assume that I described something that was pretty familiar, even if the reader had never given it those labels. I'm sure we all have some deep barely questioned assumptions in our lives and we all have at some time suffered the "them and us" anger of dualism.

But how many people, when hearing an account of positive and negative charges, of right wing and left wing politics, of hooligans disrupting law-abiding citizens, of the battle of the sexes or whatever... how many of us would instinctively ask what the *third* factor was in every case?

The correct symbol for the three-fold thinking that I wish to explore is of an *horizontal equilateral* triangle - Figure 2. It is important to bear this symbol in mind because it helps to distinguish what I consider to be true trinitarian thought from certain pseudo-trinitarian alternatives that I will describe more fully in a later section.

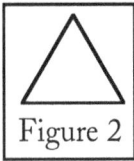

Figure 2

The triangular shape, for example, helps to clarify the distinction between trinitarian thinking and "middle way" thinking. When I said I wanted to write a book about thinking in threes, some people said *"oh yes, I always think that way: whenever I hear right and left wing extremists shouting each other down I always look for a sensible central position that takes the best of both points of view without jumping to extremes."* That is not my idea of trinitarian thought.

The equilateral shape helps to remind us that trinitarian thinking should ideally involve three *equally powerful or significant* factors, without one being either dominant over or subservient to the others.

This equality is reinforced by the horizontal placing which puts no one point of the triangle above the others (Figure 2 cannot convey this position unless you are holding the book horizontally).

So the ideal trinitarian situation is of three balanced and equal positions represented by a horizontal equilateral triangle. It is "ideal" in the same sense that the ideal dualistic situation is of two equal and opposite positions: in fact we are often "in" one side of the duality and acting very dismissive of the other side, but any outside observer would see that there must be a balance. For example, if I had spoken of communism during the cold war as "the other great system", an ardent capitalist might have reacted that there was nothing "great" about communism, it was simply a stupid mistaken notion from the brain of an idiot called Karl Marx. But it would be dead obvious to an outsider that the entire capitalist world would not need to arm itself to the teeth in order to keep out a mere silly notion - for the whole basis of the cold war was of two mighty and opposing forces. In the same way, our trinity should be of three equal positions or forces, even if we are more "into" one or two of them at any time and are therefore seeing those factors as dominant.

I hope this will become clearer with examples: because I will sometimes be introducing a third element in order to heal a duality, and when it is first introduced the third element can seem a bit trivial, lying as it does outside the emotionally charged duality. But, if it is a valid third position, it will reveal its strength and eventually be seen to come to life as an equal member of the team.

Time for an example. Let us go straight for the big one: God and Devil, good and evil, the good and the bad...

This must be about the most profound duality of all because it is drummed into us from such an early age in the form of rewards and punishments. To some extent all other dualities call on this pair for their strength: who would have bothered to take sides in the cold war if it was not for the sense that communism (or capitalism) was really deeply evil?

Now I propose that both God and Devil are dead. They are stagnant, frozen like a cold war stalemate, locked in eternal embrace. I propose that the current *fin de siecle* fascination with evil is no more than a desperate attempt to breath life into these two desiccated corpses. I also propose that breath is a useless addition to desiccated corpses: air cannot help where you need water. Water is the element of trinitarianism, so we need a third deity.

My candidate for the third deity is the Trickster. I propose that we add the Funny to the Good and the Bad - it does at least provide a title for this book. Instinctively I look for some cosmic nod of approval or recognition and I find it in certain African religions where the Trickster receives full recognition as a top notch deity. If Africa is indeed the cradle of humanity as palaeontologists are insisting, then we know that religion has been going on there longer than anywhere, so the natives must surely know what they are doing in this respect.

Indeed, once you start looking for him, the Trickster has a way of popping up in a lot of religions around the world - even if our dualistic instincts have a tendency to stick him in the same bag as the Devil. For example, the eastern concept of Maya or the illusion of existence is obviously a hugely potent force in its own right, but because of the word "illusion" we tend to lump it with a general "badness" which must be transcended. Instead, I propose, we should learn to see illusion as a vitally important third principle which is neither good nor bad, but equally necessary.

Oh hell. At this point I was planning to go all out for right-on academic respectability by breaking into pages of references to Trickster figures in art, history and religion. My inspiration was a festschrift volume called "The Fool and The Trickster" lent by a friend, but I cannot find it now.

Hello, Joel, (I know you'll be reading this because I'm going to give you a free copy in return for all the nice stuff you've sent me) don't worry, it must be somewhere on my shelves after my move, and you will get it back eventually.

So bang go my dreams of academic recognition, of readers being impressed by my thorough research and therefore seeing this as an "important" book that demands widespread discussion and a careful television documentary treatment of its ideas. Alas, I have nothing to offer you but the fruits of many years lonely introspection and I know how very little worth that has in academic circles where a book's "importance" is proportional to the employment it gives other academics in the form of lengthy references and quotations.

But perhaps the reader too is thinking "oh dear". Reflecting that, although it would have been nice to have

pages on the figure of The Fool in mediaeval England and
in Shakespeare and The Trickster in the Faustus myth
and the poems of Ted Hughes, the fact is that it is irrel-
evant personal outbursts like this rather than mere lack of
references which really condemn my work in academic
circles. It is not right to air personal problems and bitterness in the way I am now demonstrating.

Hell, I'm not bitter: of course academia must protect itself by only allowing into its ranks those who offer
work to its existing members. I fully accept the trade
union principle even when I do not subscribe to it. And if
this really was a "problem" to me do you think I would be
putting it down on paper for strangers to mock? The real
problem is to feel academically inferior and to pretend
you do not... can't you hear my laughter?

You don't know if I'm joking or not, do you? Let
that be the taste of the Trickster. Actually, having conceived the above passage I eventually found the book but,
skimming its leaden pages I opted to stick to the labour-
saving pretence that I didn't find it. So what do you now
believe?

You see, I am trying to sharpen your perception of
what I am writing. I risk you interpreting this dualistical-
ly - me and my book versus your critical ability - and you
just arming yourself with your sharpest literary and philo-
sophical weapons in order to shred the book and its ideas.
No, what I want is you to sense a trinity - you, me and this
book - and be sharp about the interactions. I have an idea
I want to put across; but this book, once written, will be
an independent entity in its own right. My idea might be
brilliant, but the book could be total crap and the ruin of

that idea. Or my idea might be crap but the book be so skilful that it leads you and many others up the garden path. Be sharp: don't assume things, we are dancing us three. If you were brought up in the duality of truth/falsehood you want to know if I am joking or not. But if you allow illusion to be a valid item (and not try to align it back on the duality as either "falsehood pretending falsely to be true", or "the truth that even the false can seem true") then admit that you have no right to know from this book whether or not I am joking - why should it tell you? The one right you have is to know whether you yourself are joking as you read it. And will you go on joking afterwards?

The Trickster can be supremely irritating because he stands outside duality rather than representing some "middle way". He is detached, and that is infuriating if you are well stuck into the duality. Let us say you are on a campaign against evil - sheer, bloody, black, stinking evil - and you come across this person who doesn't get it, cannot even see what you mean by "evil" or what is supposed to be wrong with it. Do you think that person is in the middle? No! you think he must represent an even more extreme manifestation of evil: an evil so utterly vile that it blinds us to the very perception of its distinction from good. Thus the Trickster gets shoved into the same bag as the Devil.

Anyway, having found the book I want to refer to the only personally interesting chapter in it: about Exu, the Afro-Brazilian trickster-god of the Candomble religion. The first point is that Exu, although not quite the supreme being in their pantheon, is the most respected and feared because he is seen to control everything. So, despite a monotheistic tendency to put one deity Olorun above all others, the Trickster figure still emerges as vitally important, even though his cult has comparatively few devotees.

The next point is that Exu is a god who embraces paradoxes. He is, for example, both a god of order and of disorder. This fits the idea that all existence is maya or illusion: if trickery is the basis of all we see, then trickery lies behind all order, as well as being obviously involved in disorder. Similarly Exu has both a good and an evil reputation. He has been aligned with the christian devil - partly because of his evil side and his trickery but also because he is a fire god to whom hot peppery spices are held sacred - but he is also identified with both St Michael and Lucifer. As guardian of gateways and points of transition, he is also aligned with St Peter, and as messenger between gods and men he is aligned with St Gabriel the messenger to the Virgin. Indeed Exu is said to have two hundred names because he is a character of so many sides that he is impossible to grasp.

All this illustrates well the Trickster I wish to portray. Not just a secondary figure tacked onto the God/Devil duality in order to liven it up, but another great power. He disturbs us by embracing so many paradoxes and seeming therefore to be slippery and impossible to define. That is partly because of his own nature but also partly because of the way we approach him. Any paradox is based upon two apparently conflicting notions and, because of our dualistic background, we tend line up with those two poles and exclude all else: "order and disorder? those are the only options and that trickster chappy must be one or the other... so I guess that makes him disorder". But the real Trickster lies outside this duality and has therefore apparently eluded us - while in truth it is our own dualism that has excluded him.

Now this is the weird bit: by excluding him from our "universe" of two poles we actually hand him the puppet strings. Rather like that monistic tyrant who lies in our subconscious and quietly directs our existence, the Trickster who is not acknowledged becomes the Master. In this example we are thinking "there are only two alternatives, order or disorder" and in so saying we trap ourselves into a dualistic model outside of which lies the unacknowledged Trickster. It is now his game and we are his victims trapped in the illusion of that duality: maybe siding with disorder by joining the revolution and unwittingly imposing a new order, maybe siding with order and becoming reactionaries who block organic processes of decay and therefore unwittingly create further disorder.

This, I propose, is why we are so enslaved by duality. By denying the third pole we collapse our experience into the one dimension that any duality gives us and we are trapped. We are in the game - pawns rather than players - and we hate it because we at times sense the illusion. Yet every time we get that glimpse what do we do? we ascribe the illusion to the "enemy" and are back lost in the game again.

What I want to learn to do is this: when anyone tells me about order versus disorder I want my automatic reaction to be "but what about change?". Order/disorder/change - there you have a trinity, because change is neither order nor is it disorder, though both sides will resist it and argue that it is the other. Deny change and you will be swept to and fro along that one dimension, the victim of change ever creating order in the name of disorder and vice versa. Admit change and you are now a player in a living game where disorder can be the mother of a new order, where order can order change and change change to disorder which in turn disorders order and creates change.

I have touched upon a very important quality of trinitarian thinking in that example: whereas unity is static and soothing, duality is combative and energising, and quaternity is analytical and fossilising - trinity is nourishing and flowing. I will later (Part Three) give many examples of situations where duality has energised to the point of stalemate, and I will try to show how the third principle can ease the block and revive the situation into a living, growing organism. I will also give examples of how a fossilised quaternity can come to life when informed by a trinity.

Many examples may be needed. If this idea is to come to life it needs to find a home in our minds. At first my suggestions as to how to add a third principle will probably seem like a mere "trick" of words or logic. It is, course, just that - because we are dealing with the Trickster. The point is this: do you reject it because it is a trick? or do you accept it and sharpen your perception in order to see whether it works or not? If your child was dying of an incurable disease and you knew of a quack doctor who, despite fraud squad allegations of total charlatanry, was still achieving a 70% rate of cure... would you send your child to that quack? I'm not suggesting that this is an easy decision, but only that you should be mentally sharp.

Now that I have given some idea of trinitarian thinking, let me explore one example rather thoroughly by presenting it as a story. Or, for better trickery, as a story within a story.

IN WHICH YE DUALITY IS COURTED AND RISKS IMPREGNATION BY YE TRINITY

In the outer story you are a wealthy and successful movie director who is planning your next blockbuster. However, this time you are going to go all out for critical acclaim by making this an "important" movie as well as a successful one. To do that you decide you need a Big Theme, and you choose the Problem Of Evil.

Good choice. When God (and Neitsche) died nobody took much notice. It was only when it was discovered that twentieth century humanism had killed the Devil too that people sat up in horror. Ok, God was a bit of a prig and nobody would miss him all that much because we are all pretty nice anyway. But the Devil... without him what on Earth is there worth struggling against?

So the hunt has since been on to find a new devil. Marxism, fascism, Maoism, totalitarianism... individual candidates like Saddam Hussein have offered themselves for the role and been welcomed with open arms blazing, but every time we ruined it by defeating the enemy, and thereby simply proving that they were not after all the Devil of Ultimate Evil.

By the last decade of this century things are getting desperate. People are everywhere getting passionate about serial killers, child abuse, the destruction of the environment, nationalism, Satanism... "Ultimate Evil, please come back! all is forgiven! we need you!" is the cry heard everywhere in the media.

Why so urgent? Because, however secular we feel, the fact is that our Western civilisation has been built for two thousand years upon a religion that prophesies the founding of the kingdom of Antichrist on earth and its subsequent destruction. The idea of a millennium is somehow involved: it didn't happen last time and no-one can face the boredom of a further thousand years wait, so we have only got (at time of writing) seven and a half years left to establish a decent Kingdom of Antichrist that is worth resurrecting God for (so he can hold an Armageddon showdown). Unless we do it we will be faced with the embarrassing conclusion that two thousand years of culture have been based upon a load of old cobblers. You see we did not mind God being dead as long as we still believed he was dead right. What humanity cannot face is that God could have been dead wrong.

That explains why the Problem Of Evil is a great theme for today's blockbuster, and so you decide to set it in Nazi Germany. Good choice. Dear old Adolph... ok we made the usual mistake of defeating him and so proving he wasn't really the Devil, but at least he left us a clear picture of the sort of Devil we really desire. None of that shabby old "commie" nonsense for us Devil Worshippers, please: we want black uniforms, shiny jackboots, mechanical precision and relentless drive. So here goes with the film script...

The time is the early thirties and our hero, young Fritz, is going to join the newly formed Nazi party. So, if this is a film about evil do we make Fritz a thug or raging psychopath? No way! this is going to be a real shocker: we'll make him a clean-living idealistic young hero so that his downfall will be all the more heart-rending to our audience.

So we open with Fritz, alone in charge of his dear Mother after Father died in the mines a victim of bad management by an exploitative overseas company. They have just been evicted by a cruel landlord as a consequence of being taken for a ride by crooked money lenders. "Mother Dear, I will always be here to protect you" he says as he wraps his raincoat around her skinny shoulders to ward off the beating rain which moulds the cheap cotton of his shirt close to his shivering skin to reveal the undernourished yet well-built frame of our flaxen haired hero.

Forced to fend for himself and his Mother, he goes to the city and encounters his first Nazi rally. We hear the stirring words of Adolph and we see Fritz first becoming aware and then becoming enraptured by the sense of idealism and hope being offered. At this point Art takes precedence over common sense because, for reasons unknown, the rally is being held at dawn. The scene ends to the opening chords of Richard Strauss' Also Sprach Zarathustra as we see the sun rise and its golden light illuminate the shining, hopeful face of our hero as he stands transfixed before the Nazi flag.

From here on the plot is relentless. He joins the party as a tireless worker and he sees the fruits of its success: a new spirit of hope and comradeship, better and fairer working conditions and culture and education being brought to everyone. His Mother is admitted to a shiny new flat with all mod cons.

As he rises up the Nazi hierarchy he makes some disturbing discoveries about it, but idealism and determination make light of them. He is not altogether happy about, for example, the rising anti-semitic influence and there is a scene where he explains to his friend that, although the Fuhrer must be right about the abuses made by many Jews, surely National Socialism is such a potent force for Good that there is little need to dwell upon all the petty evils in its way, because they will surely just melt away before its advance? He would far rather see the Jews relinquish their unhappy past and be welcomed into the New Order as fellows. Fritz admits that all is not so perfect with the party, but is sure that is why people like him are needed to keep it on the straight and narrow course being plotted by the dear Fuhrer.

There is a sense of growing foreboding now as the nation gears up for war. We see idealism struggling against corruption and decadence and being forced into denial. Fritz may be drinking a little and occasionally losing his temper by the time war breaks out... and he is posted to a death camp for Jews.

Of course he does not realise what it is until too late. He was not altogether easy at the term "correction centre" but managed to convince himself that it would be an opportunity to prove his point by showing how he

could bring out the true German in even the most criminal Jewish heart. Those who sought cruel solutions to the
problem would soon learn that there was a better way to
do it. Because Jews are, after all, human beings.

Fritz is in for a shock. This is the first crisis point,
and the start of his downfall - because the Jews now under
his command are no longer human beings. Whatever they
once were, the system has already brutalised them in the
fight for survival. Fritz is faced with a sullen, ragged mob
of half starved haters. In one desperate attempt to make
human contact he holds out a cigarette to a skeletal,
smelly old man. All he gets in return is suspicion, disbe-
lief - the cigarette is grabbed and the man runs away.
"Don't bother, mate" says a colleague "they are worse than
animals, they're just... disease". There is a scene where a
camp baby dies and the crazed mother turns on him and
claws at his face screaming. He beats her back in defence
and then something snaps in him: years of pent up fear
takes over and he batters her to death with his rifle butt
before he realises what he has done. We see him freeze in
horror at his act, he is at another turning point. Before
him seethes a sea of shrivelled hate-filled faces, behind
him stands his smart, well-fed colleagues applauding him
for "being a man". What a choice. He turns back and is
reassured, comforted and bought a few drinks by his
mates to cheer him up.

From there we see the new Fritz: a Nazi terror
machine who watches stony faced as the gas chambers are
filled and emptied. The only emotion he now shows is
when the words of his Fuhrer enthuse his spirit, then his
eyes once more blaze and his head is held high.

Is this then a good point to end the film? Now that we have seen the total defeat of decency and good intention? A hero turned into a monster? Is this not an incredible portrayal of the triumph of evil?

No. The film director really wants to turn the screw, and there is a whole new level of evil to explore. Let me describe the next scene.

A small dinner party of Fritz and his immediate Nazi faithfuls: quite a lot of drinking has taken place and the atmosphere is hearty and comradely. Until it is time to turn on the nightly broadcast by the Fuhrer: then suddenly everyone is solemn, attentive, devout. They sit in respectful silence as the speech begins, then suddenly the air is rent by a loud fart.

The companions freeze in open mouthed horror at this sacrilegious affront to the Immaculate Word of Hitler. One must surely be severely beaten for such a lapse? Five agonising seconds of doubt and then... a burst of unrestrained laughter. Like the first clap of thunder in a storm that has been brewing for years, that fart triggers an uncontrollable fit of mirth until they are rolling on the floor and clasping their sides in pain. One gets up and does a mock Nazi salute while blowing a loud raspberry, another does a brilliant take-off of Hitler telling a lewdly obscene joke, another takes the Nazi flag and pretends to wipe his arse with it...

Years of unadmitted personal doubts are being released in the realisation that here are a group of friends who no longer believe all this nonsense, they have seen through it and have realised where it is leading their country. The scene ends with them singing a filthy parody of Horst Wessel, a parody they learnt from overhearing a group of prisoners who had stolen a flagon of spirits and drowned their sorrows. They had heard the words and memorised them before breaking in and beating up the singers.

What is so important about this scene? It will have the audience on the edge of their seats. So far they have been sickened by the triumph of evil men, by the sight of innocent people and good intentions being beaten and gunned down. This scene, they hope, marks a turning of the tables. Now the comrades have seen through the system will they unite in rebellion against it? Will the audience, who were sickened by the sight of Jews being slaughtered, soon be cheering loudly at the sight of Nazi officials being slaughtered?

The director, however is milking evil for all its worth. Instead of this, the film will end with a new note: a note of cynicism. Our hero is next seen barking vicious orders to his young recruits, before going back to his room. There he picks up a photo of Hitler, gazes at it then spits on it, screws it up and casts it into the bin. He picks up the 'phone and orders another consignment of prisoners to the gas chamber. He puts down the 'phone and throws back his head in a cry of cold, unfeeling laughter. The film ends.

Pity the example took so long to set up. Now I must explain its object. Clearly the film is all about the Good/Evil duality, and it does no more than move down that one dimensional path to the point where Evil ultimately triumphs over Good. I did suggest a moment of banal humour where the direction might have changed, without leaving the one dimension, and Good might have made a last minute rebellion against Evil. But I also suggested that the effect on the audience would be somewhat paradoxical: as long as Evil triumphed on the screen the audience would remain good, sympathetic people; but if Good started to fight back the audience would turn into a bloodthirsty, cheering mob.

Instead, however, the film just went deeper into Evil. If it had ended without those final scenes the audience could at least argue that Fritz was not totally guilty: he was like a drunkard, a psychological victim of appalling circumstance, or a man possessed by Nazism and surely not 100% responsible for his acts? We could still believe in the earlier, idealistic Fritz lying somewhere concealed behind that brutal mask. But, with the new cynical Fritz, we are faced with an aware person who can see through all the deception... and yet he continues to act it out. That surely marks an even greater triumph for the forces of Evil?

But let us now ask what did those last few scenes *really* do? They introduced the Trickster into the duality. He entered in the form of "funny" - a fart that opened certain people's eyes - and he took residence in the form of a detached awareness of the real situation. Remember that 'detached awareness' is a Trickster quality: seeing the game. Two possible endings were then explored. In one the Trickster is appropriated by Good: that is when the awareness leads to rebellion against Evil. In the other he is appropriated by Evil to generate a new, colder and more ghastly Evil. In both cases the Trickster was kept locked into the Good/Evil duality because the film was ended before he could break out and show his true nature.

Artistically it was right to end the film there: it made a clear statement. But real life doesn't just stop in such a tidy way, so let us imagine the film running on like real life. Again we have two possibilities to explore. In the first, where the rebellion takes place, we are back in the old Good/Evil game with the Trickster laughing in the sidelines. We have all the illusion and deception of supposedly "good" people gunning down supposedly "evil" victims and so on. The other path is more interesting and will be explored further.

Here we have cynicism taking over. The effect seems amazingly evil, but I will stick my neck out and argue that this is simply because we, the audience, are still locked in the Good/Evil duality and so cannot recognise cynicism for what it truly is. It is clearly not Good, and so we see it as a puzzling and therefore sinister extension of Evil (in duality we have no option). I argue, however, that cynicism is the Trickster entering the game at the Evil end. So let us have the courage to stick with Fritz and see what might develop.

Why does Fritz spit on Hitler? Because he hates the God who has forsaken him. Why is he now so vicious with his young recruits? Because he hates them, all those innocent young Fritzes who still have their stupid lovely ideals which have long since been torn away from him. He will show them what life is really about, the little bastards. Why does he order all those Jews to death? Because he hates them too: starved, beaten sick and wretched... yet they still hold onto their damn religion, while his has fall-en in shards about him. He will kill them and kill them and kill them until they too are forced to give up all hope and die of their own accord. More rage, more laughter, more rage... but something is shifting.

All that has been bottled up for all these years has got to come out. His rage at the death of his father, the plight of his mother. His rage at seeing a beautiful dream turn sour and then collapse. When all that has come out he is left feeling utterly cold: he no longer cares. He no longer cares if the young recruits have dreams or are simply thugs. He no longer hates his prisoners and he doesn't care if they live or die. He can once more listen with rapt attention to the Fuhrer's words simply because it is all so bloody daft. He no longer cares who wins the war, everyone is equally corrupt when the pressure is on. He no longer cares if he lives or dies. He is now watching the horrors around him with amused detachment - it is all just a silly game.

At this point the Trickster has really taken over. He is no more Evil than the god who created this world and lets it all happen. Looking at the young recruits with their earnest good intentions he recalls his own youth and loves them for it. No longer repelled by the awful conditions of his prisoners he observes them cooly and notices little fragments of humanity and faith being shared right up to the doors of the gas chamber. He begins to respect and love them for it. He looks at his corner of the game of life and laments, he looks at the broader context of life on earth and rejoices. He wants to get back into the game again and feel its joys and sorrows and the sheer driving force of it, but he realises that his situation is totally grotesque.

Quite how Fritz will come to terms with his position and whether he will resign, rebel or somehow change its course is now beyond my comprehension, my control and my interest. Not that he is now a "real" person - for we are still just in the two dimensional triangle of trinitarian thinking. The point is that throughout the film we were restricted by the director's needs into a merely one dimensional world of duality: compared with that the two dimensions of the trinity seem to produce immense and unpredictable complexity. All we can see is that if we do not stop the film when cynicism enters, but allow it another dimension to run its course, then the rigid Good/Evil divide becomes a flowing, growing pattern where one can pass beyond Evil and come out laughing, then swing around again towards the Good.

The moral is that one must not be put off by the fact that the Trickster seems impossibly cold when he enters the game at the Evil end: when he enters at the Good end he is impossibly cosy, like a jolly avuncular, bottom-pinching Father Christmas. Judge him not for how he seems but for what he brings.

This example has taken very long to present, because I wanted as many readers as possible to be as far as possible drawn into the duality so they could understand or even feel the horror as the Trickster's initial cynical entry was interpreted in dualistic terms. I hope that the subsequent development indicates the value of the Trickster and of allowing the third principle to vitalise the duality, but I have some sympathy with the view which says "ok, one Nazi bastard comes to terms with his nature, but he's slaughtered thousands along the way. Big Deal." My defence is that the this would not have happened if the third principle had been admitted from the outset. Fritz grew from a one-dimensional hero/villain into at least two-dimensional humanity. If such humanity had survived at every level of the Nazi hierarchy things could have been very different. But the basic dualism of good triumphing over Evil was its own downfall.

In this story the Trickster was admitted only just in time to heal one man. To spit upon this example because it fails to eliminate the evil written into the story is like refusing to sow seeds on wasteland because they are not fully grown plants. The Trickster's role here is not to eliminate evil but to free us for new growth.

FALSE TRINITIES

This introduction to trinitarian thinking ends now with the warning "beware of imitations". I mentioned above how some people thought I was simply advocating a third or mid-way position between the two extremes of a duality. This is not my idea of a trinity. Others had the correct triangular image, but saw it standing upright so that one point stood above the other two: for them thinking in threes meant resolving a duality by seeking a synthesis which transcended it - Figure 3. Again, not quite my idea of a true trinity.

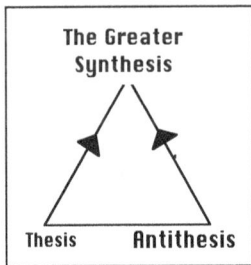

Figure 3
An hierarchical trinity

81

So examples will now be given to clarify what trinitarian thinking is not.

Most phenomena in everyday life present themselves, or are perceived by us, in analogue rather than digital form. So that when mine host at the beginning of this book spoke of women with breasts as opposed to women without breasts he was really talking of a continuum which stretched between bulging "bristols" and nearly flat chests. Between day and night there lie many degrees of dusk, between black and white many shades of grey, between good and evil many degrees of goodwill.

So it is often possible to de-fuse a duality by defining a middle course: "personally I prefer just nice, average size breasts". If a decent majority of solid citizens opt for, or at least recognise, this middle position then the extremists can get to look pretty silly - to the extent that war is diverted and there is peace in the land.

What has actually happened is that we have returned to thinking in ones: in place of a pair of opposites - tits or no tits - we have one spectrum and one truth which asserts that "breasts come in many sizes and each man has his own preference". Recognising a middle way between two such extremes is tantamount to recognising the duality as but two ends of a single spectrum of possibilities. Thus the dynamic, combative duality is replaced by a nourishing, peaceful unity.

This is highly desirable because, as explained earlier, the state of unity is a paradisiacal innocent state that we tend to yearn to return to when caught in the battles and pressures of dualism. But I also explained that duality was a necessary advance once consciousness began to cause trouble, and that any attempt to return to it can provide but short lived pleasure as long as the basic dualistic tendency is still resident in our minds.

That is why I do not consider "the middle way" to be the whole answer to dualistic battles. The trouble is that such battles, however tiresome they can become, are also very energising and can be a lot of fun. As long as you have plenty else to get on with, you can take the middle way and shrug off the lunatics who take extreme positions. But if you really get stuck into the peace of the middle way it can become a bit dull: an uneasy suspicion begins to fester that there is more fun to be had at the extremes. Who knows, maybe extremists have a wilder sex life? Then, because your middle way has neither eliminated the original spectrum nor added another dimension as three-fold thinking would do, the old one-dimensional duality is there waiting to lure you back into taking sides. It only takes an extremist to take the "if you are not for us you must be against us" attitude, and you are likely to fall right back into the game.

As an illustration of this, look at British politics. At some point in my life I became aware that the Liberal party was calling itself "the centre party", and my heart sank to my boots because I was young and crazy enough to want not just to be a Liberal but to be a Liberal *extremist*. As a centre party Liberalism lost all its glamour in the public eye to the lunatic fringes of Labour and Conservative... and as a result Thatcher came to power. I recall later, after I had already given them up, hearing a Liberal spokesman explain that they were keen to lose their "beards and sandals" image. This was in the last decade, note, a time when the entire malaise in British politics could ultimately and certainly be traced to the very shortage of beards and sandals in Westminster. (Indeed, such was the state of emergency that I would have taken a tough line and insisted on pipes and corduroy trousers too.)

To cut a long story short, we have a dualistic two party system and it is showing all the paradoxical silliness that you should be learning to expect of those caught in the game of duality. Just like the anti-Satanist christians who are more evil than the evils they seek to expunge and the Nazi party which embodied the very ills that it sought to banish from Germany, so we are faced with the ludicrous nonsense of a party which calls itself "Conservative" yet fails to put the clock back; a party that calls itself "Labour" but gets more support in universities than in the collieries; a party that claims to be anti-socialist while it strengthens the police force; a party that claims to be radical but whose main promise is that it will reverse the reforms of the other; and two parties both claiming to be liberal when it suits them and both accusing the other of being liberal when it does not. No wonder that, despite the endless column inches and hours of air time given to our politicians, they still have to spend millions on advertising agencies in order to explain to us what, if anything, they stand for or represent. Political commentators sneer at the public for voting on the strength a leader's good looks - but what else is there to vote for?

Imagine instead a proper three party system. The Conservatives could make up their mind to be conservative, so the Labour party could become radical again. Or, alternatively, they could follow Thatcher's route and align themselves properly with the "left/right" socialist duality, so that the Labour party became thoroughly left wing socialist while the Tories became the right wing or national socialist party. Meanwhile, as those two parties advocated their own versions of state control, there could be a genuine beards and sandals Liberal alternative based on the assumption that people are on the average quite nice when government leaves them alone.

I have outlined the three extreme positions which could make it far easier for the public to understand the alternatives being offered, but this is not the greatest advantage of three party politics. The biggest benefit comes from the flowing or changing quality of the trinity. Imagine in a three party system a Tory who begins to become keen on de-regulation and freedom of trade. This could be his opening for shifting towards the Liberal position. Having become a Liberal and put freedom into practice he sees that there are some people who abuse the freedom at others' expense and so he sees the point of a certain measure of state control - this is his doorway to becoming a Labour member. Putting Labour principles into action he discovers that too much state nurturing can decrease initiative and so he begins to want a tougher line... and that takes him back to the Tory party.

Now anybody might go through such a development, or any variation on it, and there is, I admit, a certain crisis of commitment each time an individual actually changes party. But the three part system would surely make it far, far easier than it would be in a two party system? Given only two parties, the act of changing party means changing *sides*: a metaphorical walk across no-man's-land under everybody's fire. In a triangular pattern you simply slide round sideways to the next position. Under our present system, going from Labour to Tory or vice versa has all the stigmata of desertion from an army, or changing sides in battle - even if you grow sick of your own party's policies you feel obliged to stay in it simply to keep the opposition at bay. There is so little sense of flow, growth or movement of ideas, at best you get reactionary "swings of the pendulum" which relentlessly define the dreary old extremes.

If, you might ask, the three party system is so much better, why did it not prove itself when Labour joined the Whig/Tory duality or when the Liberal party was a power? Why did the three collapse to two if three was so much better?

It could be because the underlying shape of our parliament is dualistic: a rectangular room in which government benches face the opposition. Now a triangular room is hardly practical - it would have dark corners where MPs might leave sweet wrappers, smoke cigarettes or relieve themselves unobserved - but I would strongly support the idea of a hexagonal, or even circular chamber divided into three zones. One would be for the party in power, one for those last in power, the remaining third for the others. In place of the inevitable "us and them" debates of a rectangular room you now have two dimensions to debate, offering a choice of patterns: at times the government could, as before, face a united opposition; on other occasions the current and last party in power could take a joint "realist" stance against the inevitably more idealistic members in the never or not recently in power sector; while at other times the results of the last party in power's policies could be faced by the combined criticism of the rest of the house. True, each of these examples amounts to a two sided debate: but at least there is permutation of groupings and further movement than in a rectangular room that rigidly defines the lines of battle.

Given such a structure there could be far more flow of ideas and solutions, and a genuine three party system might flourish. (Life being a curious and exciting game, there is also the possibility of the whole thing being one almighty cock-up which throws the nation into civil war... but you have to give me credit for trying.)

Next I want to consider and rule out a rather more subtle departure from trinitarian thinking: the one that comes from recognising its triangular structure (which the "middle way" does not) but orientating the triangle in anything other than a horizontal plane. When the triangle is horizontal it is perfectly balanced so that no one point takes precedence or is inferior to the others. But as soon as I draw my triangle on this page (Figure 4) it assumes a form of orientation based on the meaning of a rectangular page with its "up, down, forward and backwards". If I draw it with a horizontal base and other vertex upward... the top vertex looks like a "crown" over the other two. If I draw it with one side vertical and the remaining vertex to the right it suggests an arrow pointing forwards - ie two principles somehow being resolved into a third. If I draw it with one vertex to the left and the others in a vertical line it suggests one principle splitting into two. These last two interpretations are because we

87

read from left to right and so we tend to assume a progression across the page from left to right. All these are departures from the true balanced trinity of the horizontal triangle.

Up to a point these variations are all permitted because I explained earlier that the horizontal equilateral triangle was only the ideal trinity (corresponding to a proper, balanced duality); I also pointed out that we often experience our dualities in a highly unbalanced way when we are in them, and similarly we can expect

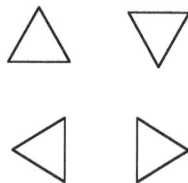

Figure 4

Different orientations on the page give different effects

the trinity to take various patterns while we are within it. Taking as example my long example of the Trickster entering the Good/Evil duality of Nazism: when Fritz is fully in the detached Trickster position he is initially *looking down on* the old Good/Evil duality as if it is beneath him, and so he is like the upper vertex of an upright triangle with Good/Evil lying along its base... But true wisdom comes as he returns to the game, but with three equal positions to play with.

So I do not object to the triangle taking different orientations as long as these are just temporary positions. My objection is to three-fold thinking based upon a particular orientation other than the horizontal. The most obvious example is the one mentioned earlier: some people assumed that three-fold non-dualistic thinking meant the ability to take any duality and recognise a synthesis which embraced and transcended it.

For example *"there have at times been battles between those who insisted that the Sun went round the Earth, and those who insisted that the Earth went round the Sun; now, however, we have the principle of relativity which shows that both positions are equally and simultaneously true"*. Now this is a genuine triangle because the relativistic position is a genuine alternative and not just a middle way between the two original positions, but it fails to be a proper flowing trinity because it is hierarchical: like the top vertex of an upright triangle - relativity is "better" and it replaces or contains the other two points of view.

As with the middle way approach, all we have done is to return to unity as a solution to the wars of duality. Yet it is a better solution because it is not boring, as the middle way turned out to be in my explanation above. The unity of synthesis actually carries the excitement of the old duality with it in the form of a sense of greater understanding or power. We return to unity, but it is a better unity than before because it is enriched with the secondary duality of before/after.

There are rich fields to explore in these orientated triangles - another orientation is the one which shows a unity splitting into a duality, eg nothingness begetting matter and anti-matter - but such logical exercises have been covered beyond my ken by Coleridge and umpteen other philosophers. So I will pass them by and re-focus on what I call proper trinitarian thought by giving an example which sails very close to the wind of synthesis at times. The subject is sex.

This is not an easy duality to extend to a trinity, but it is an important one. I dealt with the example of God/Devil or Good/Evil early on because it is such a basic duality that it lies behind many of the problems. Even bitterly fought dualities like the political Right/Left might not be so addictive or destructive if it were not for the tendency for Good/Evil to creep into the picture and take over the real meaning. Good/Evil is so fundamental that, until I had at least attempted to de-fuse it by introducing the Trickster, it could have lurked in our unconscious minds and ruined readers' perception of my very argument - I might have seemed to be trying to put across "evil" ideas, or my obvious benign intentions might have labelled me "good" and so reduced critical attention to my message.

But sex is another duality so fundamental as to present a real problem. In the first part I suggested that it might lead some readers to reject Adam McLean's discussion of the triple Goddess. I too opened the cat-flap to possible invasion by the sexual duality in my very opening example: it described male discussion of womanly attributes in a manner that could seem brazenly sexist. If this caused a reader to bristle, what chance would my subsequent arguments have of a warm reception?

The difficulty of making a sexual trinity is of deciding on a third sex. I suggest the Child.

Now, that may be a silly suggestion: so please see the following discussion not as hard justification so much as a plea for sympathetic consideration. Let us consider some of the objections in turn.

"Child cannot be a sex because sex is specifically about the reproductive process, and Child has no function in that". But some would say Child was the whole aim of the reproductive process - it is the key component.

"Child can be divided into Male and Female - as boy and girl - so does not define a third sex". But I am a man and yet I have within me both a Child and a Woman. This may actually be a characteristic of a true trinity: that each of its points must be a complete independent entity and therefore in some degree contain the other poles within it.

"Our concept of Child is not fundamental, like Man and Woman. It is a comparatively modern idea to make a distinction of this youthful state rather than see the kid as a young man or woman". Might that not just prove that trinitarian thinking is a sign of evolution beyond duality? Aleister Crowley defined three aeons in mankind - the aeons of Isis, of Osiris and of Horus, representing mother, father and child respectively together with the corresponding states of matriarchy, patriarchy and a third childlike or epicene state that he saw as beginning when the new aeon was born in 1904. He saw the childlike quality of "the masses", and the fact that political power now resided with them, as evidence of the new aeon becoming established.

"Describing Child as a third sex would open the floodgates to paedophilia and child abuse." But might it not be equally possible that child abuse is a mistaken result of our being locked into a two-sex duality while this new state of being is becoming recognised in the world?

Two-sex duality brings with it patterns of domination, manipulation and victimisation that show all the paradoxical symptoms of a dualistic game: for example the simpering victim wife whose weakness tyrannizes a marriage to its own glory, and the blustering bully husband who is too inwardly weak to face life without a victim. I see children being both victims and bullies in the family context (every Christmas the advertising industry invests millions in children's ability to bully parents) and I wonder whether their unacknowledged sexual identity is having to bear the brunt of our dualistic assumptions.

I know that there is plenty of evidence that sexual differences emerge very early and may be innate - but who can be sure that sexual stereotyping does not imprint at a very subtle pre-verbal level? Anyway, as I said before, the Child may contain the Man and the Woman just as much as my semen contains the necessary genes to create both.

Personally I found it far easier to accept the Trickster into the God/Devil duality than the Child into the Man/Woman duality, and yet the addition is beginning to take root and may well bear fruit. I note that there is a pleasing correspondence between the Child and the Trickster: a mercurial quality lies in both and suggests a cosmic nod of approval. In fact we shall find that all sorts of diverse dualities are resolved by a third element which has some qualities in common with the Trickster.

The reason I introduced this trinity was because I could draw comparisons with the false trinity of synthesis. The idea of a triangle whose points are Man/Woman/Child is not in itself radical: what is radical is my suggestion that it shows three sexes. That "family triangle" is normally seen as what I call a false trinity because there is an underlying hierarchy (in other words a duality of direction) in it. Thesis, antithesis, synthesis might seem to be the resolution of a duality (and in a very useful way it is), but I do not feel it has solved the problem of duality itself, because there remains a dualistic feeling that thesis and antithesis are the "before" state and so in a sense inferior to the "after" state of synthesis.

So also, some people would elevate Child and see it as the culmination or outcome of the Man/Woman union. Others might see it differently: a primal Child state from which springs a duality of Man and Woman at puberty - Figure 5. Both these are triangular patterns, but both have an orientation that sets them apart from my idea of a trinity of three equal partners.

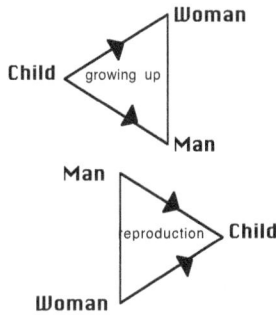

Figure 5

Two hierarchical versions: child as parent of the adult, and adults as parent of the child. neither is a "pure" family.

Sexual polarity is deeply imbedded in our nature - it may even be more basic than the primitive Good/Evil polarity - and it may be terribly ambitious to suggest replacing it with a sexual trinity. Yet the deeper any idea is buried, the greater power it seems to exert: so who knows how our lives might be changed if we began to work with this idea? What pressures might be eased in relationships if the innate combative nature of duality was enhanced with the flowing qualities of the trinity which no longer restricted me to the one dimensional game of either "being" the man or

93

"playing" the woman, but instead invited me to be part of a vital dance containing Man, Woman and Child.

There is an earnest respect in our society now for something called "the feminine principle". I share that sense of respect and even feel that my whole advocacy of the trinity could be seen as an aspect of restoring at least part of the feminine principle. I welcome that association insofar as I am hungry for acceptance for the idea in this book and will therefore lie down on any casting couch that invites me. However there is another voice which says that I must beware, at this point, of associating with the feminine principle because it is part of a duality that could swallow these, my little seedlings, with one gulp.

In the sense that unity brings nourishment and peace, while duality brings conflict and energy, in the sense that trinity brings flow and release while quaternity brings analysis and clarification - in these terms I can see unity and trinity as being Yin or of the feminine, while duality and quaternity are Yang or of the masculine. However, I hear the laughter of the child behind all this, because tradition ascribes the number one to the King or Sun and Two to the Queen or Moon, whence all odd numbers are masculine and all even ones feminine. I also note an ironical fact that those who pursue the feminine principle often are the very same ones who invoke or become (depending on their gender) angry women. Again I hear the laughter of the child in this paradox.

Without the recognition of the difference between one and three, the quest to restore the feminine can degenerate into a pure desire to return to unity, and onto unity is projected a belief that there is flow in unity.

If unity had really had flow, duality would never have been needed. If you must use the dualistic masculine/feminine language at this point, then I will add the duality of direction and say "let us not go back to the feminine as unity, but rather forward to the feminine as trinity in order that we discover more of her nature".

Can I ascribe a third sex as easily or neatly? Not really: in the next part I will consider one approach which is to agree with the ancients that there is no sex in unity; then I can recognise in duality with all its tricks and deceits the naughtiness of the child as well as its aggression; in the trinity I see my concept of the flowing feminine; and in quaternity the analytical reasonableness of the masculine. Not tidy, but perhaps it will do. After all, the introduction of the three is not an exercise in producing a neat solution, but rather in recognising the excessive neatness of duality and the need for a complication to provide solution. (Indeed, I am wary of too trite an academic dismissal of my trinitarian proposition as being itself "over-simple". That would be tantamount to saying "there are only two conditions: reality, which is complex, versus the the over-simple theories of cranks.")

However difficult these very fundamental dualities of sex and Good/Evil may be as starters, I feel it is important to explain and work on them first, because until that is done they could lie hidden and trip up all my other efforts to put across the idea of trinity.

AN ULTIMATE DUALITY?

There is a temptation to ask whether all dualities might have sprung from one original split in the unmanifest.

95

Taking a "top down" approach, an obvious candidate from a religious viewpoint would be God/Devil. A physicist, however, might suggest matter/antimatter or some even more fundamental polarity. An alternative "bottom up" approach could argue that the whole concept of duality exists only as a human construct - it is our mental model to describe phenomena experienced in chaos - and so the ultimate duality would take the form of a biological fact that imprinted itself on mankind's emerging consciousness. Here sex would be an obvious candidate. Other possibilities could be Day/Night or Left/Right referring to the symmetry of our limbs. But these latter do not have the sort of intensity of experience that I would look for in a primal, definitive duality - so my candidate would be Pleasure/Pain.

It is easy to imagine how millions of years of pleasure and pain - so closely linked within the nervous system and by the way that a cessation of pain can be experienced as pleasure, and vice versa - laid the foundation for the very deeply felt duality of Good/Evil in our primitive brains. And it is easy to see how that hard-wired notion could extrapolate beyond experience into God/Devil (Good, with now't taken out, becomes "God"; while adding to Evil the end of all Good makes "Devil" - as a crossword puzzler might put it). The only problem with this tidy biological model is that it would need to explain why such a clearly defined polarity should flip - so that Pleasure becomes associated with the Devil and Pain is deified as the stony uphill path to God. (I would like to point out, before proceeding, that personally I prefer a top down explanation in which the Trickster choreographs the Devil/God dance of life.)

So I do see Pleasure/Pain as a very profound duality with a severe grip on mankind. To me it is the engine behind all addiction. My own belief is that anyone whose only interest in, say, heroin or alcohol lies in the pleasure it can afford, such a person is not yet addicted. True addiction comes when the pleasure and the pain become inextricably linked - so that all that is not the one pleasure is felt as pain, and that the one pleasure is seen as the only resolution to any and every pain. The true drunkard needs a drink not for the fun of it so much as to relieve the pain of sobriety and awareness.

If you stand outside the duality of addiction and preach moderation and calm, you will be decried as "boring" by the addict. To the latter Pleasure/Pain has collapsed into one experience, called "Life" by the addict, at the other end of which lies "Non-life" or "Death". An alcoholic of the jolly sort will be forever trying to get you drunk to "liven you up", while someone addicted to passionate love will deny all thoughtful, kind or tender aspects of love in their zeal to "arouse real passion".

Pleasure, Pain and... what should we call it? "Calm"? "Moderation"? "Abstinence"? These form a trinity: one can flow between all three. When you know a drug or activity can bring pleasure, and you can enjoy the anticipation so much that you can withhold the drug in order to extend the anticipation; when the pain of withdrawal can be calmly accepted as part of the bargain, rather than felt as the demon that drives you back into the drug's arms; then there is hope of liberation from the duality of addiction.

I have known the wildest heights of passion, and the darkest depths of despair. I have also known intense serenity... and I have felt the siren call of addiction telling me that serenity is death and that I must hurl myself back into the fray in order to be "real" and "alive". Traditional cures for addiction recognise that the pattern is inescapable: the alcoholic never hopes to become a balanced social drinker, all that can be expected is total abstinence. The ageing hippy rock star preaches to the young against drugs: he never touches drugs nowadays, and he denies their contribution to his overall life, his awareness and his soul. Calm, as abstinence, is praised... and yet in the process Pleasure/Pain retains its hold on glamour.

This traditional approach to addiction - total withdrawal - is a retreat from duality to the peace of unity. It offers no long term hope for mankind because - as I explained earlier - duality is ever reborn from unity for the sake of its excitement.

Myself I do not want to lose the thrill of passion and despair. I believe humanity is meant to experience the ecstasy of drugs, not for ever to flee from them. Instead of wanting to cure such addictions I want to "heal" them, to make them whole by adding Abstinence as a third dynamic principle to Pleasure/Pain, allowing us to dance freely between the three. Much less would be lost this way: it might even lead to ultimate gain.

In The Book Of The Law, Hadit speaks as follows:

"Wisdom says: be strong!. Then canst thou bear more

joy. Be not animal: refine thy rapture! If thou drink,
drink by the eight and ninety rules of art: if thou love,
exceed by delicacy; and if thou do ought joyous, let
there be subtlety therein!
  But exceed! exceed!"

Superficially that might sound like the cry of the
addict demanding passion, excitement, excess. But those
words "refine", "delicacy" and "subtlety" suggest rather
that this book of three chapters, dictated by a trinity of
gods, is proposing a message more like mine (in the quoted paragraph, at least).

As in the political example (where I wanted
Liberalism to be released from the bondage of being a
"centre party" and allowed to be extreme) my remedy is to
recognise that Calm, Moderation and Finesse represent
more than just a middle course between extremes. I
demand the right to be *extremely* moderate - passionately,
even violently so.

While the addict thrashes to and fro between ever
greater extremes of pleasure and pain, his soul and his
being seem to spiral inward and collapse toward nothing.
When moderation joins the dance, might the motion not
be reversed into an outward spiral of exploration and
growth?

Just picture what chess would have been if consciousness had been locked into its duality of black and
white, so that every pawn captured was experienced as a
soldier killed, a limb severed. It would have degenerated
into a bloody stalemate like the cold war. Instead what
happened? Consciousness was allowed to step out of the

board and become the "player"; and chess evolved into an art that gives delight to millions.

And don't look back at past failures in order to refute my suggestion: I am not putting this forward as an instant cure-all potion, but as a challenge.

Is the brain-chemical process of addiction - whether to drugs, sex, exercise, love or chocolate - really a dead end or limit to mankind's progress? Is our consciousness to be forever locked within the boundaries it defines? Or is this fear just another pattern linked to our imprisonment in dualistic thinking?

Is Pleasure/Pain an absolute, or is it just another of the Trickster's games?

PARS TRES

ooooo

DE RE AERIS

One river flows from the East: it is a river of Air. Lightened by Fire we may be born aloft on its currents and view our world from the furthest empyrean. Never has so much been so visible so clearly. All lies within the grasp of sight, yet no position can seem as lonely as this Airy height.

This is a good point to look back from - as well as forward. Looking back will embrace not just reflecting on what I have written but also on what others have written on the subject of trinity.

We began in the first part with my experience of a conversation in which two dualities added up to a four-fold analysis. What I did not mention at first, and so it was allowed to remain dominant in the background, was an underlying duality of man/woman. That duality was thus left free to manipulate the reader into a sense of unease or even positive revulsion at the "sexist stereotyping" in our conversation: and this in turn could lead to a feeling of irritation at the "typically male" form of the discussion. I then uncovered the trick and suggested that we search for a less "masculine" form of analysis and I took the triple goddess as example. But the reference I quoted turned out itself to invoke some of those very divisive qualities that we were actively seeking to avoid. My suggestion was that this could be traced to the underlying duality behind our search: the assumption of a masculine/feminine divide to be crossed.

So in the second part I decided to work through the systems of thought - one-fold, two-fold, three-fold and four-fold - so that we could separate them and see them more clearly. In so doing I exposed the dualistic scheme as a bringer of discord as well as excitement, and I suggested that it had adopted the one-fold position of becoming accepted as an unquestioned, underlying assumption in our lives. I also suggested that, by making duality an absolute, we were denying the third pole to the God/Devil axis and that left the Trickster even less recognised and thus even more powerful than either God or Devil. The Trickster who holds the solution to duality remains the player behind the scenes, who keeps us victim to his illusions. Thus duality proves utterly paradoxical and absurd as well as being divisive.

By now you may again be tempted to see me as the champion of trinity over duality, so I must remind you that my championing is to restore the neglected rather than to put down the powerful. I have contrasted the "typecasting" quality of quaternity to the easy flow of trinity, but later in this part I will show how trinity not only does not oppose quaternity but rather helps it towards true expression, by releasing it from domination by duality. So trinity actually supports the four. I also would like to suggest that recognition of the trinity should go hand in hand with releasing duality from the power of unity: allowing it conscious recognition as a game to be played and enjoyed. Thus I have included as an appendix one of my earlier articles which explored the positive benefits of duality as well as its problems. Part of the process of evolving toward three-fold thinking must include learning the proper place of two-fold thinking. In my three-fold parliament example I did not seek to banish dialogue but rather to provide a more nourishing matrix for it.

Another problem which could have arisen by now is the risk of becoming aligned too closely with a campaign to create or restore a more "feminine" type of thinking - to be championing "the feminine principle" against the combative and coldly analytical tendencies of two and four-fold thinking respectively. Again I hope that this danger has been averted by my pointing out that - whereas there is a definite "feminine principle" feel to the sustaining and supportive unity and the flowing and nourishing trinity, and a definite "masculine" feel to the duality and quaternity - we must not be seduced by this if we are to avoid the Trickster's laughter. Because one, three and all odd numbers are traditionally masculine while two, four and all even numbers are traditionally feminine.

That last example introduces an important caveat before I look at other accounts of the trinity. Comparative numerology should not entail comparing particular numbers across different systems, but rather comparing the patterns within each system. I have described duality as a divisive system which brings energy and excitement but ends in paranoid stalemate. Open a traditional text which describes the number two as the number of woman and of the moon, the number of the tides, of ebb and flow, of growth... and you will understandably feel a bit confused. Twoness seems to have very different meanings - and the same may be true of other numbers when compared across systems.

Why is this so? It stems partly from a confusion of cardinal and ordinal systems of numbering. Which do you consider to be the first number? Is it one? or zero? or would you argue that consciousness and so number had no meaning before the number two and so the number "one" is merely an extrapolation backwards based on the knowledge which flows from duality? Already we have problems. Then there is a sense in which each number is the same as the one before it: represent unity by one point, and you have an object with zero dimensions; duality is two points and so defines a one-dimensional line;

trinity can be represented as a triangle and so define a two-dimensional space; quaternity can be represented by four points and these can be arranged as a tetrahedron and therefore represent a three dimensional space.

So this is why confusion can arise: Adam McLean describes dualistic thought as "one-dimensional" and he is quite right. It is no good arguing that it must have two dimensions to be properly dualistic. I intend to describe later how four-fold thinking, although usually represented as a two dimensional cross for convenience, only comes into its own when allowed its full three dimensions.

Let us look once again at that masculine/feminine contradiction. In my system as described in the last part, unity turned out in practice to be secure and womb-like and so was easily ascribed to the "feminine"; while duality was enervating and combative in effect and so was easily ascribed to the masculine. Yet the number one itself is very masculine: its shape suggests the phallic wand, the term "looking after number one" suggests a sort of brash aggression, and there is something very solar and kingly about the number itself. Whereas the number two suggests the two horns of the moon, the to and fro of tides, the rocking of a baby, the two breasts of a mother and so on. Each system is consistent in itself and follows a similar pattern, but my system is looking at the effect of applying a number while the traditional numerological view looks at the nature of the number itself. That the two should appear diametrically opposite is just the sort of paradox I expect when we found our exploration upon a dualistic assumption of but two sexes.

Bearing these warnings in mind, let us now look at some descriptions of the number three.

HOW OTHERS SEE THREE

My references are: "The Theology of Arithmetic" translated by Robin Waterfield; John Addey's "Harmonics In Astrology"; Bil Tierney's "Dynamics of Aspect Analysis"; David Hamblin's "Harmonic Charts" and the previously mentioned "The Triple Goddess" by Adam McLean.

Adam McLean describes the triple goddess as "changeable" and says how she will help us to *value a consciousness of cyclical change within ourselves*. This is very much in keeping with my idea of the trinity. However he also associates her with a uniting of the opposites in a duality and I am not happy with this because I believe this is not so much the triple goddess as the unity of a more primeval creatrix from whose womb all came. My suggestion is that the feminine is having a hard time because of such confusions: let us forget this obsession with unity for a moment and learn to enjoy the dance that duality proposed and trinity allows to happen.

The Theology of Arithmetic says *the triad has a special beauty and fairness beyond all numbers*. Nice one Iamblichus, but I must restrain myself and say I am not asking for pre-eminence but merely recognition for the three. It is pointed out that three is used to suggest plurality - early cultures only had words for one, two and then "many", so three was the same as all further numbers. There is a lot of emphasis on the sort of one-dimensional role of the mean or mediator between two extremes, and that again does not fit my view of trinity. The comparison with the waxing, full and waning moon is made, and the piece ends with a passage that does harmonise with my ideas except for that pesky unity bias again: *"They call it 'friendship' and 'peace', and further 'harmony' and 'unanimity': for these are all cohesive and unificatory of opposites and dissimilars. Hence they also call it 'marriage'. And there are also three ages in life."* I only accept this "marriage" bit if you extend to the birth of an independent child and create a triangle - otherwise we are talking of a false trinity taking us back to unity. But my main problem with the text as a whole is that it is largely exploring the number-theoretic properties of three, while my fundamental question is "if you give three things equal weight what sort of relationship arises?"

John Addey describes two as the first female number and three as the first male number, explaining that the number one is *"regarded as the unity prior to all division into male or female"*. Another complication, but it does reinforce my warning against allowing the overpowering sexual duality into the discussion too soon. He writes of three that it *"represents form as opposed to matter and it is the formal principle of a thing which makes it what it is and imparts to it special qualities."* This comes from the idea that the triangle is the first proper shape, and so three marks the beginning of shape or form which is then developed by the square, the pentagram etc - all of which can be broken down into triangles. This is a traditional idea based on exploring the geometry of the number.

David Hamblin comes much closer to my perception when he writes *"Whereas twoness is the level at which the individual realises his selfhood and therefore his separate-*

ness (self versus other), Threeness is the level at which he realises that he is not after all entirely separate, but that he has connections with the outside world." He goes on to describe how the third harmonic shows ways to explore connections and make contact, and explains that it is essentially to do with "pleasure".

Apart from the pleasure I experience of finding someone thinking on my lines, David also communicates to me that three introduces a connectedness to the divisive duality: that is quite in keeping with the Trickster being a Hermes or Mercury figure - a psychopomp who travels between Gods and humans, or the very organ of communication itself as ruler of writing and speech.

Bil Tierney (sorry about the single "l" in Bil, but it is, as they say, "for real" and not just an epiphenomenon of a sticky computer keyboard) says of the trine aspect in astrology that it *"emphasises expression that is innately creative, warming and positive in its orientation"*. He goes on to emphasise the pleasurable and lucky effects of the trine and contrasts its easiness and lazy feel with the more stimulating and self motivated aspects such as squares, oppositions and conjunctions. He explains how the trine is an aspect of relaxation and peace, but is also highly creative.

Bil's description is again in keeping with mine because the approach is similar: he is asking what effect we can expect when planets are in this three-fold pattern. But there are differences, because a trine aspect is basically between just two planets when at 120 degrees to each other. Only when a third planet forms the other point of the equilateral triangle (the "grand trine") is it a full three-fold pattern.

With these examples I have explored far enough. My conclusion is that the modern astrologer is most likely to agree with my descriptions of threeness because their approach is likely to be one of exploring the relationship or the effect when three principles are given equal weighting and placed in a horizontal equilateral triangle. Traditional explorations of threeness can be based more on the number three as an entity, its properties rather than its effect, and so come to apparently different conclusions. Another problem with other accounts is that they can be distorted by dualistic assumptions, as when the author is championing the "femininity" of the number three. For this last reason I have not bothered to go deeply into church doctrine on the Holy Trinity. I suspect that it could prove very valuable for research, but that it is an issue that has raised very strong feelings and anything said about the number three would be highly polarised by the Good/Evil duality.

In private conversation with astrologers working at the "leading edge", I have been told that the trine is increasingly seen as a "releaser or unblocker of energy", whether for good or for evil. The example in question was the Hungerford massacre when a young man flipped his lid and went shootabout with a portable armoury in a peaceful English country town. It happened during a very important astrological grand trine and surprised those who see the trine as totally benign in its influence. Isn't this just the Good/Evil duality seeping into the debate? Uncomfortable though it may seem, I suspect that the sense of pent up aggression being released by that young man may have had its moments of pleasure - his weapon collection was at last being used in a way that the weapon makers had intended, if not in a politically correct context - but the effect on the community was dire.

We now move on from lofty surveys of past views, and we aim our beaks at a few specific topics.

THE TWO DIMENSIONS OF THREE

Any two points, however placed, define a line and so define one dimension along that line - Figure 1. No other possibility exists with just two points, unless we place one on top of the other and the two points collapse into unity and zero dimensions.

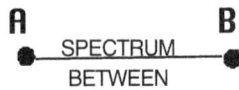

A　　　　　　　　B

SPECTRUM
BETWEEN
Figure 1
Two points must
define a unique line

Adding a third point will, in general, form a triangle and this is our main area of interest. However I must not overlook the possibility of placing the third point on the line between the other two - Figure 2. In this case we still have just one dimension but it has been enriched or supported by the addition of the third point.

A　　C　　B

Figure 2
An intermediate
point merely rein-
forces the line

This enrichment is what happens when we recognise a mid point between extremes. It leads to a realisation that there is more to the world than just black and white, we now have an infinite spectrum of shades of grey between those two extremes. Instead of two absolute principles, the number three has immediately given birth to infinity and the result is to take us back to unity. This return to unity happens because a spectrum or continuum can be seen as one thing even more easily than it can be seen as an infinite number of points. The result can be that the two concepts "black" and "white' develop into an infinite number of shades of grey which are then re-classified under the one concept "levels of light": so Black is now just the zero level while White is a fullness of light on that scale.

Most dualities can be unified in this way by adding a third principle which defines an intermediate position: hard/soft becomes "degrees of hardness"; good/bad becomes "degrees of good"; rich/poor becomes "income level". Even such apparent absolutes as male/female can become "testosterone level". This is partly why the number three has a good reputation as a balancer and soother - but in the previous section I explained why I felt such unity was not the long term solution which can be found when we allow the third position to lie outside the line joining the first two.

So let us now look at the proper two-dimensional trinity. Three points in two dimensions - Figure 3. The "two" (dimensions) gives the "three" its true freedom and that is one reason not to despise the two and imagine that the three has somehow conquered it. Duality gives trinity the gift of a duality of dimensions: thus trinity can find its true nature without sliding back into the one. The gift is the gift of freedom from the one.

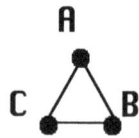

Figure 3

Let us examine that freedom. Consider the line running across the following page. It cuts the page in two,

a duality. The line is really nothing, just a cut, and it
defines only two positions (up page, down page) with

nothing in between. That is true duality in its pureness.
But now look at the line itself and give it reality: it is a
one-dimensional continuum going from right to left. It
represents duality being absorbed into the One again -
can you wonder that duality tries to resist this? The reason duality polarises us into extremists is because it is
recruiting us in its fight for survival. Born from the One
it ever risks being one-dimensioned into a continuum and
so re-absorbed into the One again. To resist this, it
inflames our hearts and encourages us to polarise into
right and left and say "those not for us must be against
us". Thus duality becomes a mind-virus and we are its
necessary hosts.

On this continuum or line there is comparative
freedom: we have an infinite number of points to choose
and can flow to and fro between the extremes, but only
as long as we are alone. If I add ten other points on the
line like so:-

then at any position along the line I am trapped between
two points and cannot escape without jumping off the
line and so into another dimension. The more points
marked on the line, the smaller the sections become and,
even though there are still an infinite number of intermediate positions, the feeling is of having less and less room
to manoeuvre.

But take a two dimensional plane: however many points you scatter on that plane I can still weave my way between them and move wherever I wish - Figure 4. Compared to the one dimensional line this feels like absolute freedom. No wonder the triple goddess offers release from duality and a sense of flow: in two dimensions we can dance.

Figure 4

Now that's what I call freedom...

So is this freedom indeed absolute? No, because the trinity has been shown to offer cyclical move-ment... and one can still become trapped into cycles. Although I can scatter any number of points over this page and still give you freedom to wander between them, just let me draw one circle on the page and I will have restricted your freedom - you are either inside or outside that circle and will need a third dimension before you can jump over it - Figure 5. Thus we find that trinity can indeed release us from the stalemate of duality and the swing of the pendulum, but it does still allow us to be trapped in circular arguments. Great freedom but not total freedom.

aaagh! trapped again

Figure 5

In 2 dimensions we are trapped in cycles, not points

The gift is indeed of freedom, but freedom is not always taken: two dimensions can easily take on a dualistic orientation such as up/down or right/left, and the power of the trinity can be restricted by this.

When planning this book I contemplated the pos-sibility of having triangular pages instead of rectangular.

Apart from the mechanical problems I decided against this because the very nature of the written word is one dimensional: a line of type runs across the page. So I decided to go for the limitations and the freedoms of an ordinary page and simply add some pictures to release me into the second dimension at times.

Under the next heading I will exploit the up/down aspect of a page by talking of triangles that are orientated. Although it means accepting a corrupt or unbalanced version of the trinity that I was earlier seeking to avoid, the point is that we should by now be able to handle this aberration. The nature of trinity is healing, and so it can heal moderate amounts of its own corruption. There is no harm in working with dualisms of the trinity as long as we have progressed to the point where we can keep the two things distinct in our minds when needed. There is no harm in discussing, say, "the feminine" in the context of trinities, nor does it even matter if we say the trinity is feminine, as long as we remember that this is not absolutely true and we are only talking about overlapping aspects of two very alive and vital concepts.

SEX AND THE SINGLE TRINITY

Let us look at the triangle, but let us also allow ourselves to be influenced by the page it is drawn on, and so distinguish directions.

John Addey described the traditional aspect of trinity as the giver of form. How does this arise? One point is just a dot of infinitesimal size, it has no shape or form. The true duality, as we saw in the last bit, is just a cut in unity so it becomes two parts. The duality itself has no shape. Even if we envision it as a line, this is a sort of non-shape because it has no area. But the triangle is a definite, clear shape. It is the first and clearest shape. Add a fourth point and you get a whole range of possible shapes - square, diamond, rectangle, bent quadrilaterals - and all can be broken back into triangles. So on with five and higher numbers - Figure 6.

This is why the three is associated with form: it is the first to describe a shape that can actually contain something: namely the "inside" of the triangle. This containing aspect is another reason for the "feminine" feel of the trinity. I will choose the magical image of the Cup as its symbol, because it expresses the accepting and nourishing aspect of the

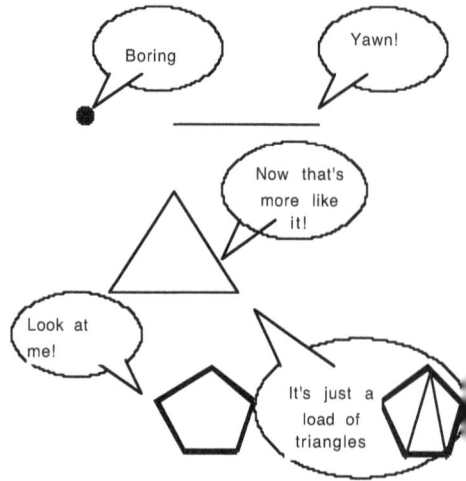

Figure 6

Three points gives the first 'real' shape. After that it's just more and more triangles.

trinity, its ability to contain something and to allow it to heal or work itself out. Draw the triangle point downward - Figure 7 - and this cup-like quality is illustrated: we can see a triangular vessel into which liquid can pour and be con-tained.

This symbol is indeed somewhat "feminine", so let us explore it. The downward pointed triangle is the alchemical symbol for water, a "femi-

Figure 7

The cup as symbol of a 'feminine' triangle

nine" element that needs the cup to contain it. Whereas the upward pointing triangle is the symbol for the "masculine" element of fire which rises upwards - Figure 8.

This sexual distinction comes from allowing the duality of direction up/down. The downward triangle also suggests the

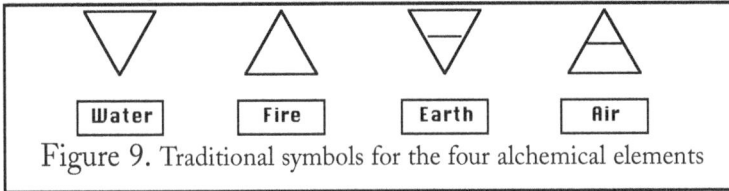

Figure 8
The 'masculine' triangle

| Water | Fire | Earth | Air |

Figure 9. Traditional symbols for the four alchemical elements

woman, whether it is seen as the shape of female pubic hair or whether it is seen as the trinity of her sexual organs - two breasts above and one vagina below. The upward triangle similarly suggests the male, whether it is seen as the upward point that is typical of male pubic hair (which has a more pronounced line up toward the navel), or whether it is seen as the trinity of male organs - two testicles above which rises the erect member - Figure 10.

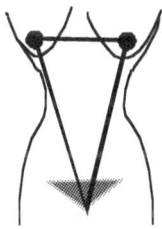

The greater and the lesser feminine triangle

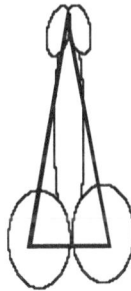

The masculine triangle

Figure 10
The triangle as sexual symbol

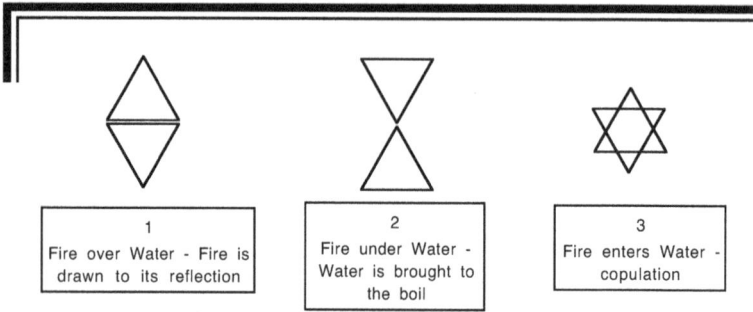

1	2	3
Fire over Water - Fire is drawn to its reflection	Fire under Water - Water is brought to the boil	Fire enters Water - copulation

Figure 11. Seduction as a magical formula

These two symbols when combined provide a medium to explore formulae of sexual magic. Consider these three versions of the hexagram - Figure 11. the first is of two triangles base to base, the second is of two point to point, the third is of two superimposed to form a true hexagram.

These three images illustrate the formula of seduction. The first picture is of the man and woman standing close to each other: he is taller and so his upward pubic triangle rises above her downward triangle. It is a picture of fire over water: this is when the male fire sees its reflection in the still waters of the female - projection of the male's anima in effect - and the male desires the female intensely.

The second picture is of foreplay: his up-thrusting triangle is now aimed at the base of her pubic triangle and is stimulating it. Fire is now beneath water and, like a stove on which the kettle is placed, the water is being brought to the boil.

The third picture is of the union or copulation of the two elements: the male triangle has penetrated the female. It shows a hexagram which is a magical symbol for the completion or perfection of the work.

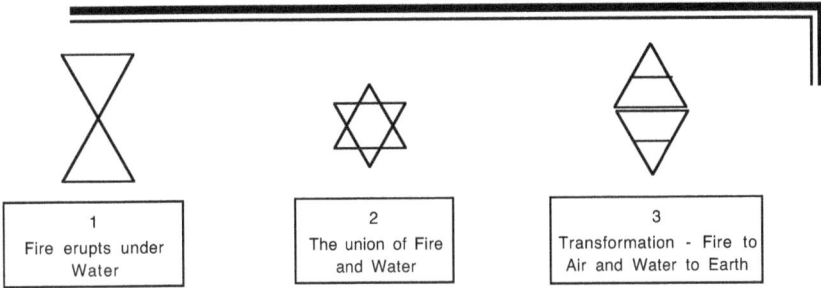

1	2	3
Fire erupts under Water	The union of Fire and Water	Transformation - Fire to Air and Water to Earth

Figure 12. Marriage as a magical formula

The next set of pictures begins with the two tri-angles point to point, progresses to the hexagram, and ends with the two triangles altered slightly and now base to base - Figure 12. This is not so much the formula of seduction as the formula of marriage or partnership. It begins with the male fire being an excitatory element that stirs up the female water: this is the symbol of the young aggressive male disrupting the female's peace. Then we have the symbol of union which is the marriage ceremo-ny. Then we see the two triangles base to base but they now both bear the mark of having been in the hexagram: each has a line across it. This mark has transformed the symbols: the upward triangle of fire now has a line and this makes it the alchemical symbol for air; the downward triangle is similarly transformed into the symbol for earth. Thus the watery young woman has become the earthy mother provider, the base upon which the male is now established. He is no longer the fiery warrior but has been domesticated into the airy communicator who goes between the home and the world to bring wealth and food back to the family.

I won't extend these examples further, they were simply an illustration of how we can admit duality into the picture of the trinity without ruining it. There is much to be learnt by meditating on orientated triangles. As to the object of such meditations: it does not do to be too specific because their value depends upon the individual. This book advocates the trinity and with it a certain mental approach which we have symbolised by the cup. If you, the reader, form a cup-like acceptance instead of a sword-like critical frame of mind, then certain things will accumulate drip by drip within that cup and you may choose to give them value as they mount up. You cannot collect liquid on a sword or a scalpel, it flows around the blade and is gone. "At least I wont be taken in by a load of rubbish" is the defense of this sword-like approach, but it is a truly insecure defense, because the cup of acceptance allows matter to accumulate but never forbids its later analysis. It is fear which says that one must never take on anything except the verifiable truth or the hardest fact because otherwise reason's blade will rust and you become a dupe. The fact is that a whole lot can safely accumulate in a cup, it can be kept sealed in an alchemical athanor and its contents allowed to mature and come to life. Then the dragon's egg is broken open and... yes there is danger, but that is why we now need our sword to be at the ready. Now is the time to decide if the dragon is offering healing or destruction.

Too early use of the sword instead of the cup lies at so many troubles. I have here described simple sexual patterns in symbols - do they offend? To see these simple patterns is to open oneself to deep respect for the institutions of seduction and marriage. But what if you hate marriage? Then any wise soldier would advise you to respect your enemy. Marriage brings a load of problems, it is itself a huge problem: to this the dualistic sword would respond by insisting that non-marriage must therefore be the solution... and suffering singles proliferate. The trinitarian cup, however, tells us that non-marriage is no solution, but simply a more interesting problem. With that realistic viewpoint you can gain a little more pleasure from being single.

Again, the profundity and universality of these symbols provides only a warning and not an interdiction to those who seek other formulae. If you are gay or wish for different sexual roles, then mere rejection of the traditional formulae is not so effective, because the harder they are chucked away the harder they eventually hit back. A better technique is first to study the pattern of the traditional role and see where its undoubted strength lies, then a revised pattern can be created to suit your needs while incorporating as much of the existing formula as is required or is tolerable. And if nothing is tolerable, well at least you know what you are up against.

TRINITY AS CHANGE

Both the number two and the number three are traditionally associated with the idea of change or flux. The number two expresses it in essence - with its association with the horned moon and the ebb and flow of tides between high and low. While the number three, I suggest, expresses it in practice with its ability to unlock the stalemates of duality in the everyday world.

Pure duality has no shades of grey. It offers just two off and on extremes and the only possible movement is a switch to the opposite. This is hardly movement at all, but it must seem very exciting after the state of unity which has absolutely no movement. It is the addition of the third intermediate point which defines states in between the two extremes and so allows linear to and fro movement: the tide flows because there is not just two positions of high and low tide, but the inbetweenness continuum to be passed through.

But if instead you give the third point an independent position off the line, you have a triangle and the new possibility of change which runs from point to point around the triangle - creating a cycle of manifestation. While a pendulum or the tide can only move to and fro, the Moon has a different aspect when waxing, waning and Full: she defines a continuing cycle of time.

Linear time or cyclical time? Along one dimension time can only flow along a line from the past toward the future. But allow two dimensions and time can run in cycles: Spring, Summer, Autumn, Winter; waxing, full, waning; day, dusk, night, dawn; birth, maturity, death and rebirth. Some would see a conflict here, the idea that linear time is "masculine" and cyclical time is "feminine" and that the modern belief in the former has made us insensitive to the nurturing qualities of the latter. Does not the belief that death is the end of everything make us grasping in life? while belief in the cycle of rebirth would make us more caring?

Beware, the masculine/feminine duality is creeping in again, and once more the Trickster is pulling the strings. You see, the idea of cyclical time was actually stronger in the days when our indicators of time were linear - ie the candle or the hour-glass. But for centuries now our indicators have been cyclic - ie the round face of a clock that runs through 12 hours and begins again - and yet the idea of linear time has become dominant.

We are now, however, being subjected to a third form of time - ie digital time - which is neither linear nor cyclic but discrete. It is in essence most like the hour glass, except that now one witnesses each separate grain of sand click past until all is gone and the glass must be started again. If linear time is Masculine, and cyclical time is Feminine, is this digital time not that of my third sex the Child? Because it is a time made up of discrete moments: every unit recorded is the "present" and there is no sense of movement between. In digital time we live forever in the present - my computer says it is 16:47 and a moment later it is still 16:47 - and like massless information we are suddenly dropped into another present where the last digit has been incremented by one. Time is now made of present moments each as long as our attention span, it no longer flows but hops.

But to return to the sense in which duality is rigid and requires a third principle to unlock it. Even in real life examples like Left/Right politics where the inbetween stages are recognised we still find a tendency to stagnation as both sides arm themselves into deadlock. My suggestion that this was a corruption: not so much innate in duality as in our hunger to return to unity. Given that there are, say, two systems of politics which we call the right and the left, there is a tendency not to embrace joyfully the opportunities for play that this situation presents but rather to try to restore unity by getting rid of the other pole. Having decided that we are, say, Right, we are tempted to deny the validity of the Left and try to elimi-nate it. But you cannot rub out one limb of a duality in that way because the opposites are so intimately reflected in each other. What happens when the Right wing tries to stamp out Left wing influences is analogous to what happens when you try to cut off the South pole of a mag-net to create one which only has a North pole: you get a shorter magnet which still has North and South poles - Figure 13. What is worse, the shorter magnet means there is less spatial dis-tance between the poles: you have brought the unwanted South pole closer by trying to get rid of it. Do it again and it comes even closer; again and it is closer still. Those Reds, once safely in a far evil country are now right under your bed and as active as ever, so you fall into catatonic fear:

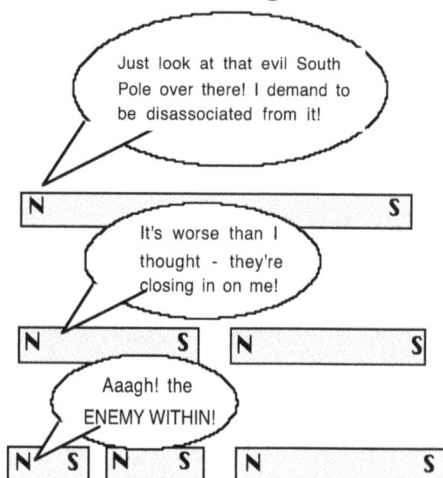

Figure 13
The problem of evil

sitting on your bed with a shotgun over your knee swear-ing you will get them... there is only one place left for them to hide now, it is right in your own mind. The enemy has ended up truly "within", and all has frozen over.

There is wisdom in duality, but it requires us to acknowledge it in its entirety and play the game. The reason this happens so seldom is perhaps because it is not easy to do - until you have discovered the third point or Trickster from where you can survey the board properly rather than fall right into it.

So perhaps, as an extension of this principle - we will also learn more about the three as we now reach forward to explore the four.

HAIL TO QUATERNITY IN ITS RESURRECTION

My story began with the development of a four-fold scheme: Mother, Daughter, Amazon and Witch. I later expanded to a general look at fourfold analysis and I concluded that, although a great aid to clarity, it is always prone to typecasting and fossilisation of ideas. Having seen some ways in which trinity can help duality to flow, let us now see what it can do for quaternity.

I approach quaternity with the utmost respect because, for all its apparent faults it does represent what is in a sense our highest evolutionary achievement: namely analytical philosophy and science. Saying that, I very much hope that other even greater achievements lie ahead, but merely wish to pay tribute where it is due. I myself am prone to four-fold thinking as the opening story revealed, and I based a whole theory of magic upon such a scheme (see SSOTBME - An Essay On Magic).

So fundamental are these number concepts that in a sense all four-fold schemes are the same, just as all dualities can be seen as variations on the God/Devil game. So let me take a very well worked example as my basis for discussion: the quaternity of the elements Earth, Air, Fire and Water, to which have been ascribed the four magical weapons or tarot suits being respectively Disks, Swords, Wands and Cups.

A first warning: though my scheme is in accord with the majority view, some would ascribe Wands to Air (seeing the wand as a tree branch or reed) and Swords to Fire. This is a healthy reminder that there is a degree of arbitrariness in all such symbols - that is precisely what gives them room to come alive whereas precision would merely ossify the system.

Let me illustrate this arbitrariness and flexibility further. We have a quaternity of systems now made up of four types of thought: one-fold, two-fold, three-fold and four-fold. As suggested earlier, there is good reason to ascribe three-fold thinking to the Cup as symbol. So what of the other ones? Does not the number one suggest the Wand? and the power of unity suggest the sceptre as Wand? And for the duality that cuts unity into two and creates division and war, what better symbol than the Sword? That leaves the Disk for the quaternity, and that is not bad for the number of the elements representing manifestation, stability and Earth.

Quickly, forget it! Although a system could no doubt be based on that scheme, I changed my mind. Ascribing Unity to the Wand was a bit like the scheme which saw the number one as male - it was based more on the number itself than upon its effect. This scheme also put the two masculine elements Fire and Air at the beginning and the two feminine ones Water and Earth later: thus it was more a statement about the linear evolution of manifestation from ideal, through concept, then feeling to matter: a sort of precipitation from the unmanifest. I wanted a more balanced and typically four-fold scheme rather than this linear sequence of four. (This scheme was equivalent to the trinity that simply places the third point mid way between the other two).

So I instead chose the Disk or Earth to represent the stability and the nourishing quality of Unity. Then the Wand or Fire represented the line with which Duality parted Unity; its straightness symbolised the one dimension of Duality and there was also the magician's wand symbolism to reveal the trickery or illusion which lies behind its play. As before the Cup or Water portrayed the Trinity with its ability to contain flow and heal. That leaves the Sword of Air to play its traditional role as the weapon of reason and analysis by representing the Quaternity - more the scalpel than the battle sword. Quite a different scheme, but one which is more in accord with the present treatment of the symbols.

So let us return to the four weapons or elements that can be arranged in the traditional four-fold way as in Figure 14.

This is the traditional cross of the elements in the Western mystery tradition and it fits well with psychological observation: Water is the element of Feeling and it opposes Air, the element of Thinking. Fire is the element of Intuition and it opposes Earth, the element of Sensation. Thus we notice how human relationships often polarise into battles between Air and Water, with one partner being cool and reasonable while the other is gushing with emotion, (and yet the roles have

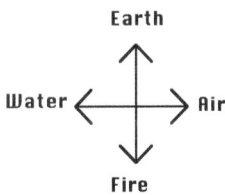

Earth
Water ← → Air
Fire

Figure 14
Traditional cross of the elements

a way of suddenly reversing in a typical polarised fashion as discussed in the essay "Stress Analysis Of A Twisted Knicker" in Volume II of Ramsey Dukes' collected essays). Similarly there is the polarity between the fiery idealist and the pragmatic realist, in which the idealist despises money and material values but his life is totally dominated by lack of it, while the realist denies all idealism yet ends up being swept along by money for its own sake rather than as a means to pleasure or fulfilment (ie finance has become idealised into an end rather than a means).

This four-fold pattern in its various manifestations is so familiar that it would seem to be beyond question. So let me question it. Is it really right to place Fire and Earth as opposites? Ask the man in the street which element is opposite to Fire and he might well suggest Water - and with good reason. And the two remaining - Earth and Air - are quite arguably opposite too, because the original duality of creation was formed by Gaia the Earth Mother and Uranus the Sky or Air Father. So here is a new scheme for the four elements which fits our four male archetypes rather better because it places the Father (Earth) opposite the Boy (Air) and the Poet (Water) opposite the Warrior (Fire), where they surely belong - Figure 15.

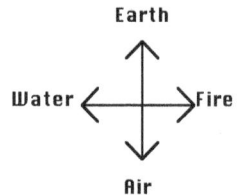

Figure 15

Elemental cross of the archetypes

So our supposedly clear and sensible quaternity has gone a bit haywire, being able to be laid out in two distinct and apparently conflicting ways - prompting the dualistic response "which is correct?".

But at least we can console ourselves with the thought that no-one would be silly enough to suggest that Fire and Air were opposite, or Earth and Water - as in Figure 16. Would they not? In fact this is the scheme used by what must be the greatest majority of those using the four elements symbolism - namely the astrologers.

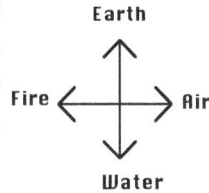

Earth

Fire ←――――→ Air

Water

Figure 16
The elements of astrology

In astrology the Air signs oppose Fire signs, and Water signs oppose Earth signs - and a very satisfactory and workable arrangement results.

So we now have not just two ways of arranging the elements but three! Does this make a nonsense of the scheme of four elements? Or should we take the number three as a clue and ask the trinity to come to our rescue?

Remember how in an earlier section the number three failed to produce the real goods until we allowed duality to give it two dimensions to play in? So I am suggesting that the number four is failing us at this point because we are imprisoning it in two dimensions where we should give it three.

So let us jump out of the page in our imagination and put those four elements onto the four vertices of a tetrahedron as in Figure 17. Now they occupy four equal and independent positions in three dimensional space.

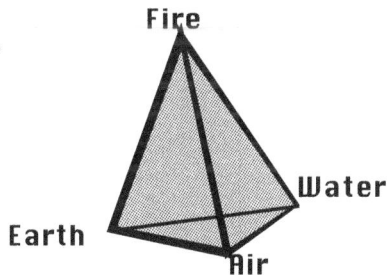

Fire

Water

Earth

Air

Figure 17
The elemental tetrahedron

129

What is more, nothing has been lost. Without dismantling the tetrahedron, you can get back to that classical cross of the elements simply by turning the tetrahedron until it is viewed edge on. From this angle it appears as a square with the four elements at the corners in the old familiar two-dimensional layout. But the intriguing thing is this: rotate it so that a different edge is toward you and the arrangement is now different. In fact all three apparently contradictory arrangements mentioned above are found to be just different viewpoints of the one tetrahedron - Figure 18.

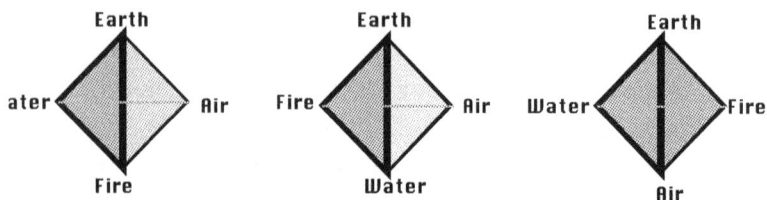

Figure 18. All the arrangements are but different views of the one tetrahedron

Now this I find interesting: the four-fold system of the elements which is so familiar was found to be a bit suspect in two dimensions, there were three contradictory arrangements possible and that seemed to spoil the tidiness of what is meant to be an neat analytical scheme. It was like having three contradictory scientific theories for the same phenomenon. But when we introduce the third dimension we create a new scheme in which those three contradictory two-dimensional schemes are seen to be just three viewpoints of the same fundamental layout. I like this tetrahedron of the elements, let us see if we can do more with it.

How about ascribing the four archetypes met at the beginning of the book to this tetrahedron? There is a slight problem: I have difficulty deciding which female archetype belongs to which element. The Mother seems very obviously Earth, until one asks if there should not be something of the healing Water, and of course there should. Ascribe Water to the Witch in the obvious way and I wonder then what has happened to the Witch's knowingness and detachment which belong to Air (without detachment Water cannot manipulate because it identifies too strongly). By symmetry that should make Air the element of the Amazon, but surely she also has the drive of Fire and the practicality of Earth.

This is a bit worrying, so I had better go for the male archetypes that seemed to fit the elements more clearly than these female ones do. The Warrior is Fire, the Poet/Priest is Water, the Father is Earth and the Boy is Air: it gives us a tetrahedron with those four archetypes at the points - Figure 19.

Now the resolution of the female archetype problem could be this: let those four female archetypes be represented by the faces instead of the vertices of our tetrahedron of elements. So each female archetype is given not one but three elements. Taking the polarity of Father and Daughter we would expect these two to be opposite each other. That would make the Daughter a creature of Air, Fire and Water. That seems to fit my perception of

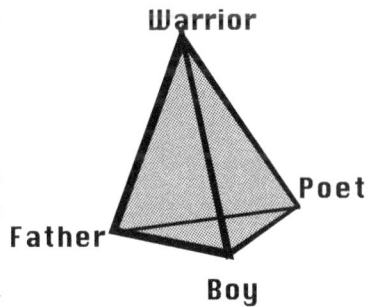

Figure 19

Male archetypes

131

the archetype well: as well as the obvious childlike Air we have the willfulness of Fire and the Emotionality of Water - Figure 20.

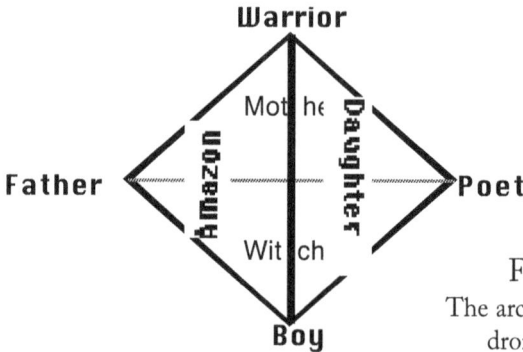

Warrior

Mot he

Amazon

Daughter

Father

Wit ch

Poet

Boy

Figure 20

The archetypal tetrahe-
dron completed

Taking the Mother/Boy polarity would mean that the Mother has the elements of Earth (the provider and base), Water (the tenderness and nurturing) and Fire (the warmth and the protective drive). The Poet/Amazon polarity gives the Amazon the elements of Air (intellect), Earth (practicality) and Fire (drive and idealism). The Warrior/Witch polarity gives the Witch the elements of Water (feeling), Air (detachment and cunning) and Earth (the dark Crone or limiting aspect).

Whereas the male archetypes are distinguished by being one pointed, representing just one element in its raw state, the female archetypes are more rounded and complex. You could say that these female archetypes are distinguished more for the element that is missing and which seeks its completion in the opposing male arche-type, while these male archetypes seek the female that would offer them this complementary role..

Thus the Amazon is the archetype which is complete apart from a lack of relating (Water). She can stand alone and survive without a partner. If she does have a sense of incompleteness it is best answered by the worshipping Priest/Poet who provides the Water. The Mother is the archetype who lacks detachment (Air) and she torments herself trying to pin down the Airy puer aeternus figure of the Boy. The Witch is the archetype who lacks Fire as energy and drive, and she harnesses the Warrior to translate her dreams into action. The Daughter is the archetype that lacks substance (Earth) but can always find a Father to provide it.

Personally I find this arrangement very satisfying and very fruitful for meditation. Have I indeed discovered a more satisfactory way to describe these female archetypes by giving them three elements, or would another person have a different idea? One possibility strikes me as follows: would a female reader rather ascribe three elements to the male archetypes and just one to the female ones? In other words: am I right in seeing the female archetypes as more complex? Note that my scheme makes each of these four goddesses a triple goddess with three elements and that would seem to ring true.

Or is it just that, as a male myself, my inner experience of the female archetypes is richer than a woman's? Whereas a woman would have a richer experience of the male archetypes and might see more depth and complexity in them than I do. To her the female archetypes might be one-pointed while the male ones were complex. It is true that male archetypes are more irritating to the male: we snigger at herculean warriors or Rambos, we consider the poet/priest a bit wet, we crack jokes about fathers in Volvos and show envy/contempt for the playboy. In the same way the female archetypes irritate the woman with their suggestion of an unmatchable "ideal" in men's minds. However, I am encouraged by a scheme which reveals each female archetype as a Triple Goddess - and I wonder how you all feel about it?

There is another thing to notice about this tetrahedron of the elements: stand it on the ground and it gives us a triangle of three elements and one other which stands above those three in space - as illustrated in Figure 17. (This "orientation" of the tetrahedron is equivalent to the orientation a triangle is given when drawn on the page, as discussed earlier.) Whichever element stands above depends how you place the tetrahedron on the ground - as does the way the three elements on the ground are orientated. This suggests an interesting departure from the fourfold scheme of the traditional magic circle.

In nearly every branch of the Western mystery tradition, as well as such schemes as the Red Indian Medicine Wheel, the four elements are ascribed to the four directions in the form of a cross. This has already been illustrated in Figure 14 where Air is to the East, Fire to the South, Water to the West and Earth to the North - Figure 21. This is a familiar scheme well implanted into the consciousness of witches and magicians around the world and

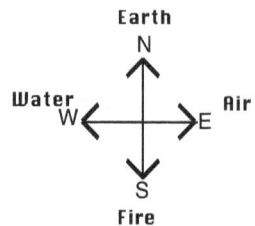

Figure 21

The Medecine Wheel

so I would not want to disrupt it overmuch - but why this four-fold scheme?

The answer would typically be this: the Sun rises in the East, is hottest in the South, sets in the West and is at its nadir in the North. All very basic and natural you might think. Rubbish: anyone really in touch with nature, as these witches are meant to be, would tell you that there are only two days of the year when the Sun rises in the East and sets in the West - namely at the Equinoxes - so by all means use this magical cross on those two days, because it is highly appropriate. However, in the Northern hemisphere in Summer the Sun does not rise in the East but more like the North East; it is then at its zenith in the South and sets towards the North West - and you cannot see it at midnight so what the hell where it is?

That would suggest that our Summer magic would be better based on a circle which did not contain a cross but rather a triangle of elements which is fixed by the Fire point being to the South with Air towards the North East and Water towards the North West - as in Figure 22.

That means Earth is missing from this circle but, according to our tetrahedron, it is has its own position above the cir-

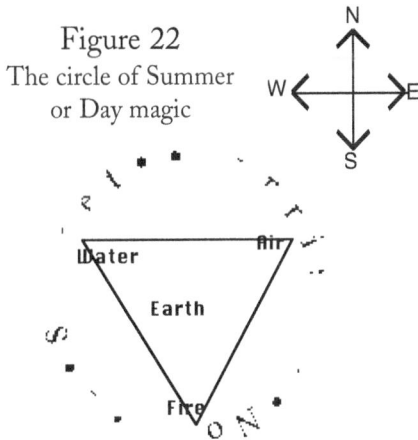

Figure 22
The circle of Summer
or Day magic

cle: is it therefore in exile or is it in a ruling position?. It could be represented by a symbol placed on the altar in the centre if you wish.

This is the circle for the daytime or Summertime magic of light: there is of course a Winter of darkness triangle which is fixed by Earth being at the midnight point of North. In Winter night begins with the Sun setting in the South West, so Water is there, reaching its nadir in the North, for Earth, and finally ends with the Sun rising in the South East, the point of Air - Figure 23. Here the missing element is Fire - appropriate for the magic of Winter and darkness - and again it could be seen to play a special ruling role above the circle or in the centre.

In this way we develop a new magical system which respectfully retains most of the old tradition and yet more truly reflects reality. My suggestion is that this scheme might bring with it the virtues of the trinity: instead of a fossilisation of magical tradition, a new flowing, growing system for the coming Age. This idea will be explored more fully in the final section where we look at practical application of our several trinitarian explorations.

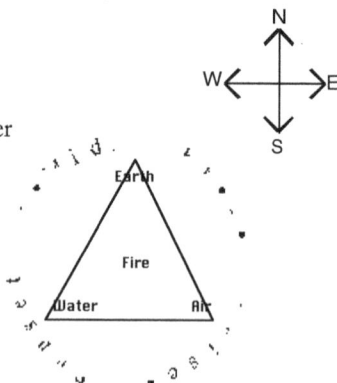

Figure 23
The circle of Winter
or Night magic

136

PARS QUATTUOR

ooooo

DE RE TERRAE

One river flows from the North: it is a river of Earth, most heavy, cold and stub-
born to my senses. This is the river from which all is born, yet nothing is born
by it. Its only flux is imparted by its children, who bear its leaden weight upon
their shoulders. Woe, woe and far to go.

Alas my son, if I could but demonstrate one jot or tittle of benefit that the world could garner from these speculations, inner labours and phantasms of my imagination, then would this book, my gift, be worthy to lay at your feet. But should I fail in this task and discover in this text no more than some tumour of diseased reason and wayward dream, then what am I offering but a plate of mental excrement made soft by sweat and tears? Less than nothing would this gift be if the receiver felt obligated by society's derision to dissociate himself from its author, close the door and toss away the key of that lumber room whose contents are his only inheritance from a sorry parentage.

Oh well, here goes. This is the part where the waffle needs to prove itself not for its ability to stir emotion, nor to intrigue the imagination, nor to satisfy reason with its tidiness, but rather for its capacity to provide some courses of action and practical benefits.

A word-processor corrects so cleanly. I wrote "provide solutions" in the last sentence then decided to delete the word "solutions" so over-used by today's (Thursday) information technology marketeers. As you will by now be aware, I am a creature of Fire and Air and most happy to be carried on clouds (many years past membership of the British Balloon and Airship Club, though yet to go up) so I do enjoy those sort of gatherings where concerned and intelligent people get together to put the world to rights. But some people expect too much of words and feel disappointed or frustrated on these occasions. These are they who stand up and ask for some "real solutions" to be generated in place of all this talk of nice ideas.

It occurred to me the other day that what they are really asking for is something solid to emerge from the discussion. Now that is not a solution, it is a precipitate. The process of solution takes what is hard and dissolves it to a flowing liquid, whereas precipitation is the process by which something solid descends from that medium.

In that sense this book, then, has already provided its solution. Trinity, or the addition of a vital third principle to the rigid structures of duality, is the principle which dissolves rigid form and creates a flow. In place of hard, polarised positions it gives us a circle dance of manifestation. That is the solution.

In this section, however, I want to try my hand at precipitation. Oh dear, what chance is there of success? During the three weeks labour of writing this book (time drawn out by power cuts and kinky software bugs that ate my words) I have earned absolutely nothing, have hardly answered any mail, have neglected the garden, my friends, my family and my health. Who the hell am I to claim anything but torment from these ideas? The precipitation, my friends can only show itself in your lives, and not on these pages. All I can now do is to set the process in motion.

ESTABLISHING THE TRINITY

In describing thinking in ones, I explained how a new idea seems to take a generation or two to filter down to a state of more or less unconscious acceptance; and until that has happened the idea can never be terribly effective.

Later I suggested that duality is firmly established as such an inner tyrant, and it is from this position that its power is wielded.

So my problem is that this poor old trinity is not going to work many miracles until it is thoroughly accepted in your minds. And why should you accept it until I have demonstrated some miraculous benefits to justify the considerable effort of adopting a new type of thinking?

Oh dear, an impasse.

The only thing to carry us over this impasse will be faith. Jesus and I (after suitable negotiation) have decided to adopt different strategies on this matter: he turned down the devil's offer early on (during his 40 days in the wilderness), while I have been waiting and hoping the devil would make me such an offer: that is why the subject has only just been broached. No miracles suggested so far - I suspect the recession is being felt in Hell too.

While on the subject... may I try a slight diversion to put off the dreary practical bit? It is generally assumed that the devil of one religion is the god of the religion that was overthrown by it. Thus our Christian devil has the horns, hairy legs and cloven feet - as well as the chthonic style - of the old Greek Pan whose death was announced with the establishment of christianity in that land. Pan, meaning "All" was a supreme deity revered in Pagan times. Similarly, the horned god of the witches we are told has been overthrown and demonised as another ingredient to a christian devil who - if we are to judge by the word of the Bible (and those who speak much of the devil would not have us judge by aught else) - never took such a clear and recognisable form in Christ's own day.

A similar tendency for the god of old to be dethroned and become the devil of the new can be traced by comparative mythology in many lands, and it raises the question as to why anyone would bother to go on worshipping a disgraced god once a new one has been installed? The usual answer is that the devil tempts one to worship him by offering easy reward. The image is presented of the new religion's stony uphill path of virtue in contrast to the old religion's smooth downhill slope of pleasure and vice.

This is not a total red herring: You see, I am suggesting that we might indeed have to put a bit of effort into establishing our trinity. Do not expect instant gratification: establishing the trinity could be hard work - a stony uphill path. Compared to it, duality could play the devil: because it is comfortably installed in our unconscious assumptions it could well offer a much more easy and seductive view of reality.

I am suggesting that this is the mechanism of God/Devil changeover: the new god needs to fight for his throne in the face of an established inner tyrant. That is why religions can play so dirty when trying to get established. They have the disadvantage compared to the old god who is like software already installed and commissioned in the minds of the people: hence the need to call the old god "devil" and denounce his user-benefits as illusory. If you cannot see how serious this problem is, ask any small-company computer salesman who has ever pitched against IBM.

Of course, the real interest in all this is to ask when is it Jesus' turn to become the devil? Now some would claim that the new religion has already come in the form of rational humanism. I am sure the humanists would uneasily endorse my analysis as they count the empty seats in the South Place Ethical Society and contrast it with the vast wealth and brouhaha being raked in by visiting christian evangelists. Jesus is megabucks in the States and his solutions are being sold as easy. Isn't that just what we expect from the devil? A religion that brought us the Jonestown Massacre, that divides Northern Ireland and many other parts of the world, that supplies a steady flow of child abuse cases for page three of the Telegraph, and a religion that makes the cash tills sing. "Satan's Jewel Crown" has already swapped heads.

Now rational humanism would no doubt see this little book from its Olympian heights as a sorry piece of mumbo jumbo and dotty speculation, and would no doubt have the power to banish my efforts into the darkest corner's of the Copywrite library toxic intellectual waste disposal operation. Therefore, in the name of my new god Trinity, I ask you to fuck rational humanism, put on your fawn skins, take up your thyrsi and read on like a pack of crazed animals.

Here goes for the stony uphill path, Ravers!

TRINITY SOFTWARE - INSTALLATION GUIDE

The object is to make trinitarian thinking a natural, almost automatic process.

At present dualistic thinking operates like that. When someone says "we must unite in the battle against evil" the automatic assumption is that the speaker must consider themselves to be on the side of Good. Out of a zillion possible principles - Relativity, Entropy, Beauty, Digitization, Nihilism, Surrealism, Neo-Impressionism, Post-Natal Depressionism etc - we just automatically assume that it must be Good or some imitator of Good that is raising the banner as soon as the enemy has been identified as Evil.

Now trinitarianism is not necessarily going to open the floodgates to all the possibilities suggested above, it will simply enable us to ask if the battle is going to be one of morality or mockery. Good or funny... well at least it's the beginnings of choice.

If my intuition is right, the benefit that we can look forward to is that this new way of thinking could offer solution to some of the dualistic tensions in our own psyche - as will be suggested in the following section. Now, we all know that it is far easier to put the world to rights than to sort out one's own self, therefore the installation process is going to focus on well-known dualities in our society to start with. The sort of work already begun as examples earlier in this book, but this time I will be hunting for particular signals or patterns that could give some clues towards the generalisation of the process.

It was suggested that the Good the Bad and the Funny was a suitable starting point because the God/Devil duality is surely one of the most fundamental and pernicious dualities of all. If only I could depose the assumption that life is a battle between Good and Evil in favour of the assumption that life is a circle dance between the Good, the Bad and the Funny, then this book will have justified itself.

But be careful. I am not saying the latter view is "good" while the former is "bad". By all means go to battle if you have been given a Rambo kit for Christmas - with camo bow, survival knife and headband. Just don't feel you have to.

Consider the Trickster figure again: the suggestion is of a mercurial, detached, deceptive, clever, funny, maddening, stimulating, liberating, communicating and healing nature. Some of those qualities, such as healing and liberating, may be not so much his own intrinsic nature as the result of his role in completing the trinity. But, in another sense, he is so fundamental that I would identify him with the trinitisation process itself and say "yes, he is a healer".

When I considered the difficult sexual duality, I came up with the Child as third sex. The fact that Child-as-sex seemed in accord with a good number of the qualities ascribed above to the Trickster, was a sign to me that I could be on the right lines.

What about the political example? Insofar as both Right and Left wing politics seek to create a State that compensates for the defects of the individual (the proper attention of the Left being to nurture the weaker individual and of the Right to channel the toughs) then a Liberal viewpoint which states that individuals are basically OK if left alone, does have that sort of child-like innocence. And to talk of the Liberal party during the run up to an election does seem to be a formula for inexpensive laughter, so maybe we can indeed see some of the Trickster nature again at work? (Or maybe not: perhaps instead it is the Monster Raving Loony Party that is the vital third force needed in British politics.)

Often the initial impression of the third element is that it is "detached". This again may be just the initial subjective impression as we are lead away from the battlefield, but it could be a helpful indicator. Notice in particular the way the Trickster nature was revealed in my long-winded Nazi tale: he was at first mistaken for an even worse evil until we had the faith to follow his trail.

Consider this example: what is the opposite of love? Most people would say "hate", and it is certainly a good candidate because love and hate seem to entwine in the way that we expect of polar opposites in a duality. But it is surely possible to argue that love and hate are not truly opposite because they are both strong feelings, and that "indifference" is the true opposite of love. However, following the path we have thus started on, we could equally argue that indifference, like love, is also a human feeling and so we need to find something even further removed in semantic space. "Washing powder", for example, is arguably more opposite to "love", because it is even further removed from it than "indifference".

As this example grows batty it draws attention to the fact that opposites are ill-defined unless we state, or at least accept, a universe of discourse. Those who describe hate as the opposite of love are assuming that the universe of discourse is "human passions". If we extend the universe to embrace all human feelings then indeed indifference becomes the opposite of passionate love (and, at the same time, the opposite of every other intense passion).

HATE

The true trinity of Love Hate and Indifference. Each is equal and independent

LOVE INDIFFERENCE

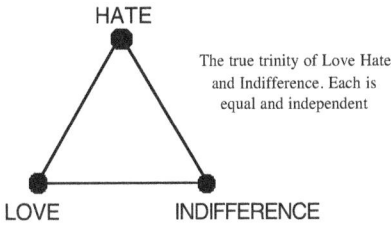

COLLAPSED TRINITY 1
Hate is projected out, Love and indifference merge within as Niceness.
This is the formula of "Wooly Liberalism"

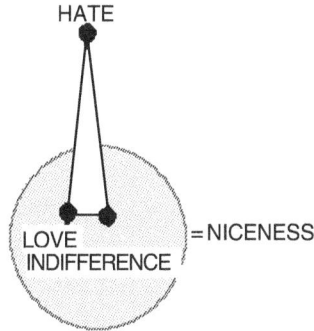

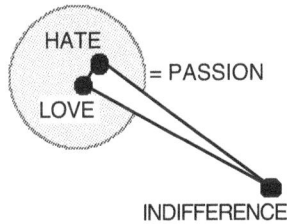

HATE

LOVE
INDIFFERENCE } = NICENESS

HATE
LOVE } = PASSION

INDIFFERENCE

COLLAPSED TRINITY 2
Indifference is projected out. Love and Hate unite within and are called "Passion". (This is a victim state insofar as Passion is the opposite of Action.)
The formula of Tragic Romance

COLLAPSED TRINITY 3
Love is projected out. Hate and Infifference unite within.
The formula of Psychopathy

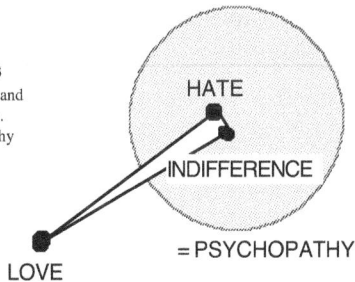

HATE
INDIFFERENCE

LOVE = PSYCHOPATHY

Figure 1
How a healthy trinity collapses into pathological duality

The object of this example is to point out that an examination of the assumed universe of discourse can often provide clues as to the third principle we seek. Someone locked in the Love/Hate duality can be like the addict locked in a Pleasure/Pain duality described in an earlier section. Blowing hot and cold in relationship, such a person jeers at calls for moderation or calm in the way an alcoholic jeers at the temperate or moderate drinker. As described for the alcoholic, they will collapse Love/Hate into one quality called "passion" and champion it against anything else which they term "Indifference" or "Death". By the formula of this book, however, we can see that all human feeling are part of this universe of discourse: in which case the duality of strong feelings - Love/Hate - is completed by Indifference as a third principle. When this third principle is accepted, then both love and hate actually improve. To hate is added the whole new armoury of snubs and ignoring, and to love is added a whole new dimension of gentle, non-passionate loves which can provide necessary breathing space in the closest long-term relationship. I love, for example, the summer sweet air I am breathing now, but I am so glad that the closeness of my relationship to air allows me to be indifferent to it for long periods as I concentrate on writing these words. In pauses I turn my attention back, fill my lungs and sigh ecstatically: air is my dear love and supporter, and I campaign for its cleanliness. And I preach the airy lightness of love as being just as important as the fiery onslaught of passion.

Mind you, I cannot guarantee that there always is a third principle - it was a bit of a struggle to drum up the Child as third sex, after all. If you take some duality like East/West, what on earth could the third be? The answer here is that East/West, insofar as it is just a clear definition of direction, is not a problem duality that needs to be healed by a third principle, but as soon as the words take on further meaning they allow the possibility of resolution. For example: during the height of the Cold War, East/West became a livid duality between communist and capitalist systems, just the sort of situation demanding release. Then the term "Third World" was introduced and it did a good job of reminding us that there were vast areas of the globe where that choice of political systems was of secondary importance compared with the need to survive. There is not much of the Trickster quality in that example, except perhaps that Third World countries were often sufficiently detached from the superpower battle to be able to play it as a game to their best advantage - pitting Russia against America in quite a Trickster manner.

Armed with these clues as to the sort of qualities expressed by the third principle, let us press on to new examples.

OTHER COMMON DUALITIES

One person says to me "why can't you just relax and watch television some evenings instead of worrying about all those things you're supposed to be doing?", while another says "whenever I pass you seem to be watching television, how can you run a business with so little effort?".

That seems like two opposite poles in the Work/Play duality - one exhorting me to play more and the other to work more - but both agree that the television is an instrument of play. Not quite so: for years I have lived without TV: I only got one when I became seriously involved as a copy writer and felt the pressure to keep my finger on the pulse of public dreams. Just as a company director would scan the Times, especially the financial pages, as a pleasure but also in order to "keep abreast of what's going on", so does my job require some awareness of public fantasies and fashions and the TV is a good indicator of that. Thus the situation is not so clear as those two people believe.

The fact is that, although their views seem to be diametrically opposed, they both agree that work and play are opposites: the one says that I am working and so cannot be playing, and the other says vice-versa. To me this opposition is not really entrenched: I never had such strong motivation to "get away from it all" on holiday because I try to make every day of my life have some of the quality of a holiday. To live a life that needs to be got away from seems to be gross error. My work involves a big element of play, and my very favourite forms of play have a way of being quite productive. That is the third attitude: but how to I put it into a single word? Should I say that the third factor which resolves the Work/Play duality is "Being"?

The snob versus the inverted snob: as in the last example we have two people who initially seem to take diametrically opposed views, but on inspection they are found to be utterly united in their belief in a class structure on which everyone is neatly positioned. The person who notices your little finger crooked as you hold your teacup and says "I do appreciate these little niceties of the well brought up", and the person who instead says "for fuck's sake drop that ghastly affected upper-class mannerism": those two are both reinforcing exactly the same belief, namely that the crooking of a little finger puts one in a socially higher class. All that is different is the alignment relative to the Good/Evil axis.

So the third position could be the one that sees the crooking of the little finger as simply a reflex response to the problem of supporting a hot cup by a rather twee little handle, rather than any weighty matter of education or breeding. That a preference for crystal goblets over drinking wine from a can could be more to do with sensuality than any code of deportment.

Quite often things that are "classy" are actually more sensually satisfying - linen sheets have it over nylon, cashmere suits over crimplene, smoked salmon over most fish fingers and good manners get you more strokes per slap - but it is as if some innate puritan guilt requires us to deny this and instead justify the preference in terms of some abstract "quality of breeding" or "refinement of taste". Then, by the same token, a revolution is started against those same preferences and sensual pleasure gets lost in the battle.

The problem is very similar to the Work/Play example above, and in both cases we found a solution by looking at the shared belief of the opponents and considering an alternative to it. "Detachment" is the common Trickster quality in the resolution, though the nature of my suggested solutions is quite different. In the previous example the resolution was more idealistic than the original duality, in this example it is the snob and inverted snob who are living in idealistic models while the resolution is more a question of sensual awareness.

If it were not too much like the last section I would suggest a diagrammatic model of this. Given a two dimensional plane with two contrasting points on it, there are exactly two equilateral triangle that can be constructed on those points as base - Figure 2. Note that the two possible new vertices (A) themselves form what could be a dualistic pair of opposites.

So let me replace the idealistic "the ideal work should be play" attitude of the last example with a down-to-earth one of "I don't care whether you think it work or play, I just do what I bloody well feel like doing". And let me replace the sensuality of this last solution with the idealised notion that "one should be able to appreciate certain things and people in their own right without needing a class structure". There, two new solutions - but can you really tell the difference?

One man's solution might speak a different language to another's, yet be very much the same in principle. And perhaps when we get to more personal problems we will not be restricted to two dimensions: there may be an infinite number of solutions out there - Figure 3 - and my solution might not be at all the right one for you.

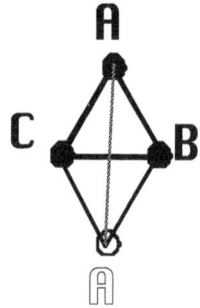

Figure 2

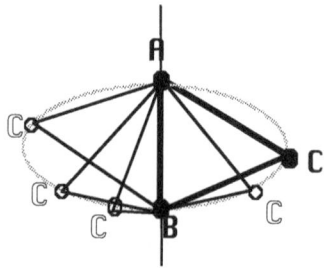

Figure 3

In three dimensions there can be any number of third points

That last example, though easy to resolve for me, suggests another example that is far more tricky: it is the problem of a class system itself. Following the last example you might think the class system was like any other duality: toffs versus plebs. But that is only in the black and white snob/inverted snob world. For most of us the system has a major difference with the other dualities considered, because in the one-dimension of class hierarchy nearly everyone is in the middle.

This can produce a curious topological variation from the other patterns I have examined, insofar as it sets up a new duality of "middle class or not". The game consists of trying to prove everyone else is more middle class than oneself. So if, for example, one knows a manual labourer who does all the right things like wiping his nose on his sleeve, dropping aitches and eating peas with whatever you are not supposed to eat them with, then catch that man listening to an operatic aria on the radio without immediately re-tuning to another program and one can instantly label him as "impossibly middle class". And exactly the same thing could be said about HRH Queen Elizabeth II if one found Laura Ashley curtains in a private room at Buckingham Palace. What is happening here is that, everyone having retreated to the middle ground, the dominant duality is no longer Upper/Lower but Ordinary/Extraordinary with a desire to prove that everyone else is ordinary.

This makes the class system a difficult problem to tackle by my method, and quite an instructive challenge. On the one hand there is a genuine Upper/Lower distinction and that is a bit like the North/South duality - a straightforward distinction of absolute directions and not therefore open to resolution. On the other hand there is a bizarre duality which has turned into Centre versus Extremities.

Rather than just look for a third principle, my plan here is to simply ask if we can make the one dimensional hierarchy of class extend to two dimensions. There is this tight little ladder of increasing poshness - getting a job, getting your own flat, then your own house, your Ford, then your Volvo, then your Mercedes, then your Ferrari and so on - and yet there are those who stand outside that ladder and are able to make the climbers feel uneasily outclassed. These are the people who arrive in a battered 2CV or Land Rover wearing frayed clothes and yet still seeming to make the earnest climbers look absurdly gauche and vulgar.

I've got it! *Education!* That's the Trickster in the God/Devil of the class system. The Oxbridge/Public School graduate who does the most vulgar things yet makes them seem impossibly classy. As with the other Trickster manifestations, this is the figure which stands outside the class system and yet runs the whole game. I have taught at Eton college in the late 60s and seen young men denouncing class while in the process of becoming it. Hermes, the Trickster, is also the god of education.

Does that mean that we should banish education in order to eliminate the class system? No, for that would just collapse it into a one-dimensional ladder of increasing wealth, a much tighter class system with less scope for irritation and fun, and more scope for anger and hatred.

Until I hit on the Education Trickster just now I was expecting to resolve this duality more on the lines of Parkinson's law of traditional class cycles in Britain - Figure 4. Here the "plebs" emerge from the womb of London and begin an upwardly mobile journey via Essex and the East side of England until the family creates an industrial empire in the North of England. Here the family achieves nobility and the children are first educated at

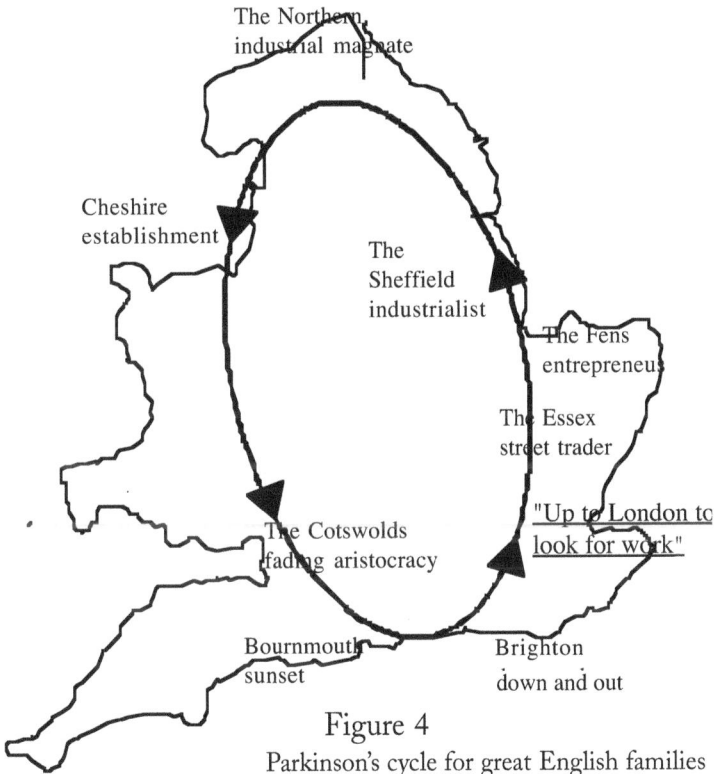

The Northern industrial magnate

Cheshire establishment

The Sheffield industrialist

The Fens entrepreneur

The Essex street trader

"Up to London to look for work"

The Cotswolds fading aristocracy

Bournmouth sunset

Brighton down and out

Figure 4
Parkinson's cycle for great English families

public school and Oxbridge. That marks a sort of apogee of worldly effectiveness after which the family begins to migrate South via the Western side of England as the family fortune dissipates. Thus Cheltenham and the Cotswolds becomes the point of maximum class accretion but rapidly shrinking wealth. Like a limp balloon the family sags to the South Coast resorts and turns to drink, the class rubs off and the next generation return to London as down-and-outs to find their fortune... and the cycle begins anew.

That model of the class system has the cyclical and two dimensional quality I look for. It seems to replace the rigid Upper/Lower model with a trinity of Rising, Falling and Being There. But my feeling is that this model simply confirms the trinity I have just discovered: Education is the Trickster which bursts the balloon of rising wealth. The proud industrialist, who has earned his brass from muck, sends his children to Eton and Roedean where they learn to laugh at social climbers and the work ethic. The hydrogen of wealth begins to leak as the champagne corks pop and the Trickster plays a merry jig...

Countries that boast of "no class system" have the inflexible hierarchy of wealth, but it is true that they do indeed "lack class". One manifestation of the Trickster is the god Wodin in the Norse tradition: he has a way of appearing as a scruffy tramp and heaven (sorry, Valhalla) help anyone who scorns him in that guise. *The Rolls Royce speeds past Cardboard City and a tramp is heard muttering a latin quotation on the follies of material accretion...*

Natural or Artificial - that's a pretty busy duality nowadays, judging by the advertisements. If a bee uses highly sophisticated bio-technology processes to convert nectar into honey within the laboratory of its own body, this is deemed "natural". While if ICI uses a vastly simpler process to create a sweetener it is deemed "artificial".

In this duality Man is seen as opposed to Nature. It began with Nature being the winning side and Man a poor naked creature struggling against these great forces; now Nature is the poor helpless lady, symbolised by the dying butterfly, that is retreating before the onslaught of mankind.

It hurts a bit to write that, because deep down I feel it is true. Perhaps this example belongs in the next section on personal dualities, but it is sufficiently universal to stay here.

So here is a duality and we look for the tell-tale signs of paradox. Yes, of course, Man is itself a natural phenomenon and in creating technology it is being true to its own nature. Nature, with Her ice-ages and earthquakes, is capable of the grossest acts of vandalism that make even the automobile seem like a minor irritant on the face of the Earth.

So here we have a typical game dualism, with all its attendant dangers - typified here by the sort of grand global scheme to avoid environmental disaster which turns out simply to precipitate a different environmental disaster.

Now this is not an easy duality for me to resolve because I am a bit too much in it still. All the better, therefore, as a practical example. Taking the last example where Education proved the key, I suggest that Ecology is the key to this one.

If that seems too simple and suspect, I suggest that this is because we are in a similar position to my imagined audience in the story of Fritz the Nazi in part II of this book. Remember that when the Trickster first appeared he seemed like just a worse form of Evil - because his humour was seen as cynicism. I explained that the Funny can be kidnapped and projected by both the Good and the Bad, just as both Right and Left wing governments grab and then deny the Liberal label.

In this case Ecology is still seemingly trapped in the duality of Man/Nature. To those on the side of Man against Nature, the ecology movement is just another pack of bloody animals needing to be herded up and shot. While, to those heavily into Nature against Man, ecology is just a fashionable label used by industry to justify its latest inroads into Nature. My suggestion is that this ambivalence could reveal a true Trickster potential for Ecology to be the third principle which resolves the ancient Man/Nature duality. To do this it will have to mature to a truly holistic discipline that recognises not just Man but also its works as part of Nature.

Note my rather feeble use of the neuter "it" for Man in conjunction with the usual "she" for Nature - it was, of course, just a token gesture to keep this example disentangled from that old Masculine/Feminine duality again. Once the association is made of Man, Evil, Technology and Masculine all versus Nature, Good, and Feminine, the duality is so rock solid ingrained that the Trickster will be forced to set light to himself and be shot from a cannon before he is even noticed.

In that last example we saw how lining up the natural/artificial duality with the good/bad duality corrupted the former. That alignment is totally arbitrary: man/nature has nothing to do with good/bad.

If you consider each duality as a one dimensional spectrum between two extremes, then those two axes should really be orthogonal, ie at right angles to each other - Figure 5. I deduce this from the fact that it is just as easy to project "bad" onto nature (as some previous generations have done) as it is to project "good" onto nature (as modern and earlier romantics tend to do).

Ideally every duality pair should be orthogonal to every other to define a clear space of discourse. If two axes coincide it simply means we have two pairs of names for the same duality. If two make only a small angle with each other, it signifies strong parallelism between the two, and one should seek to isolate the orthogonal component in order to clarify the distinction.

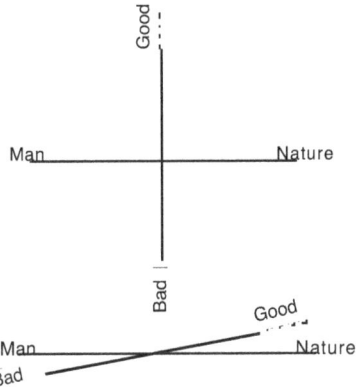

Figure 5

Above: the two dualitles acting independently and fairly.
Below: the Man/Nature duality is being corrpted by its closeness to Good/Bad

Sorry, that theoretical explanation should belong in the last section, so I will instead go ahead with an example of a duality which really does seem to lie close to the good/bad axis. Then we will try to see in what ways it is independent of it.

The example is nice/nasty - an example I understand well because myself I am a classic "nice guy".

As a nice guy I tend to attract nasty guys. An obvious factor is that I am too nice to tell them to push off and so I end up lumbered, like a sort of sink drain trap, with the guys no-one else can put up with. But the real reasons are deeper. Nasty guys are fascinated by my niceness in a sort of love/hate way. They recognise a serenity in me that they wish they had and, being nasty, they get angry that I have it and they do not. That anger confirms their nastiness and, because my presence is somehow involved, the anger is directed at me and I become the victim of it and that makes me look even more the nice guy - which in turn makes them even angrier and so nastier. Thus the nice/nasty duality becomes polarised in the nasty guy's mind and aligned with good/bad.

Imagine a relationship on these lines: an angry woman attracted to a nice guy, finding herself even angrier and so becoming even nastier. Sooner or later there will be such ructions that they will go to a marriage guidance counsellor. The counsellor will naturally like the nice guy - because that's what a nice guy is all about - and that will annoy the nasty guy who will then lose her temper and bully the nice guy in front of the counsellor. The counsellor will then recognise that they are a nice/nasty couple.

There is no problem in the counsellor recognising the nasty guy's nastiness, as long as it is not seen as being "bad". The one most likely to see nastiness as "bad" is actually the nasty guy herself. That is the mechanism for her anger: the nice guy makes her feel bad. So she will be angry because she thinks she now looks bad in front of the counsellor, and she will assume that even if the counsellor is being even handed.

Now the duality game begins. Feeling bad, she wants to feel good, and the way to do this is to make the goodness of the nice guy seem worse than her badness, so she will seem good by comparison. So something happens just like the "cynicism" factor in my long example of Fritz the Nazi (Pars Duo): she assumes that the nice guy is actually putting on a nice act in order to ingratiate himself with the counsellor and make her look bad. That makes the nice guy *really* bad whereas she is merely being honest and open and so, by comparison, really quite good.

Again we have now a full blooded duality game with all the paradoxical signs. Here is the nasty guy believing herself bad at one level and forever trying to prove others "badder" in order to convince herself that she is good. If she sees a TV documentary about the Chinese invasion of Tibet she will be understandably grieved about the cruelties inflicted on the Tibetan people. But when the Tibetan non-resistance is shown, and the Dalai Lama is seen saying that he bears no grudge against the invaders, she will not reduce her own grudge against them in order to keep pace, but rather become even angrier against the Chinese for being so cruel to such a gentle people. She is locked in the nice/nasty duality and maybe cannot see that the Chinese might be angered by the Tibetan tolerance and see it as a slimy trick to win the hearts of Westerners against their justified cause. They too might feel bad about their nastiness and translate that into "being made to feel bad".

As in the case of Fritz, it is the imagined new extreme of evil which holds the key to the resolution once one recognises it as the third principle showing. In that earlier example cynicism was seen no longer as a greater evil, but as the intervention of the Trickster. Here I suggest that the idea that the nice guy could be pretending to be nice introduces a third principle which we could call the actor or player. So you now have nice guys, nasty guys and actors. The parallel between the actor and the Trickster is as obvious as the parallel between nice/nasty and good/bad.

As in the case of cynicism, I must now demonstrate that the actor is truly independent of nice/nasty.

It could be a nice guy playing nasty. Imagine a nice guy schoolmaster who looks into the school chapel on the eve of term end and finds some leavers superglueing the Headmaster's minicar to the ceiling of the chapel. Maybe the HM is himself a nasty guy and the schoolmaster feels real sympathy for these naughty kids and reckons it's all a jolly jape, yet he decides that for the good of their souls he must storm in pretending to be furious at such behaviour and report them at once.

Or it could, as suggested earlier, be a nasty guy playing nice. The defensive assumption of the nasty guy when cornered is that everyone else must be as nasty as themselves, but some of them are either cruelly repressed and dare not show their anger, or else they must be so nasty that they put on niceness in order to deceive. The problem with this theory is as follows: there is only one way to pretend to be nice, that is by being nice. You see the oily salesman who wines and dines you in order to trick you into buying a leaky yacht is actually being nice insofar as he is making you feel good and happy. Admit this is true, but just don't jump to the conclusion that his being nice means that he must be good and therefore to be trusted to sell a good boat. It's that last assumption, that nice/nasty is the same as good/bad, which causes the problems and makes you look back in anger and label his former niceness as "wicked deception".

In any case, the idea that nice and nasty can be mere roles instead of absolute qualities does help to release them from good/bad and allow us to see them as independent descriptions.

I recall a highlight quote from an article on motor racing in a woman's magazine, it read something like this: "who wants a New Age wimp when she could have a Latin motor-racing bastard!". My first feeling was that the writer was kidding herself: if you manage in any sense to "have" him rather than be "had", then he is no true bastard. But I also recalled a song by Dory Previn about two contrasting loves in her life *One was a poet, and one drove a truck: the one would make love, and the other would fuck*" and the song ended *"But the one that was gentle hurt me far more, than the one who was rough and made love on the floor"*. Sounds like the typical pain of a nice/nasty affair, and it does suggest that the writer of that article on motor racing, having suffered the pain of having a nicer New Age partner, could now be fleeing to the emotional security which comes from knowing that your partner is the nastier one; and, rather than admit to flight, she was consoling her ego by pretending that this retreat was a bold revolution against New Age principles.

This dilemma was explained properly in Shaw's "Man and Superman" where the heroin turned down the nice, adoring worshipper and instead wooed the harsh and critical man. She explained that she had no hope of living up to her image in the mind of the worshipper, whereas the man who despised her presented on the one hand a challenge, and on the other the comfort of knowing she couldn't possibly be as bad as he made out that she was.

One of the characteristics of nasty is the actual belief that nasty equals bad, whereas nice guys are usually the ones who understand that nice does not mean the same as good. As a nice guy one has probably faced teenage ridicule for being nice, with the suggestion that nice is somehow not sexy - another arbitrary linking of dualities - the nice guy also recognises how niceness may generate anger in others.

Since the 80s there has been a growing tendency to see niceness as bad. This is just as foolish - imagine telling the Dalai Lama he mustn't be so nice as it might make some Chinese soldiers and politicians feel bad! It would be like forbidding one to carry a knife in case others hurt themselves with it - niceness is not good or bad, it must be recognised as simply a survival technique which happens to bring pleasure to many at the cost of pain to the few. Morally it is on a level with hunting deer for a village feast.

Myself I see nice/nasty as a duality within the old fourfold scheme of the humours - choleric/phlegmatic and melancholic/sanguine. Of those pairs the former is nasty because it contains the angry people and the self indulgent (who won't lift a finger for anyone else), whereas the latter is nice because it contains the people we feel sorry for and those that cheer us up. For reasons suggested above, the one group attracts the other and it causes problems in relationships unless both partners realise what is going on. The nice guy initially feels melancholy guilt and assumes that it must be their own repressed anger that is causing the other to be so nasty. Meanwhile their own natural niceness is exactly the quality that is begins to look to the nasty one like slimy ingratiation - an attempt to steal the limelight and make others "take their side". Good/bad has then taken over the duality.

Not unrelated to the last example is the duality of wanderer/stay-at-home. As the song goes *"Hitch up ma pony, saddle up ma ole' grey mare - Ah'm a stranger here, Ah'm a stranger ev'rywhere"*.

The wanderer drifts into the small town, scruffy and travel-stained with all his possessions in one small bag and a guitar over his shoulder. The girls cluster around as he sings about the big wide world out there, and they fantasize. Meanwhile the boys next door are saving up for wedding rings, and are furious with the bum.

The wanderer somehow seems cool - nowhere is big enough for him except the whole wide world. Ask him about life and he can gaze into the distance and say something cool and cryptic, and he doesn't stick around long enough to have to prove it true or live up to it.

Compared with him the stay-at-home seems dull, prosaic and small. But the wanderer who is adored and worshipped by the town girls feels that no-one really loves him, and that is why he has to keep moving, because he imagines that real love is when you have been married for many years and have got a stable family all around.

This wanderer/stay-at-home duality lies behind the relationship between America and Europe. Americans tend to give out that "big 'n easy" feeling because their culture was founded on people who packed a few possessions and set off across the seas to find a new life (Australians have a little of it, but tempered by the many who were forced to go there). No wonder the best images come from American songs: *"Ah'm a rambler, Ah'm a gambler, Ah'm a long way from home - If you don't like me you can leave me, an' Ah'll ramble alone"*. That song does not conjure images of the British Ramblers' Association in kneebritches and anoraks.

As pioneers it is ok for Americans to express aggressive feelings like confidence and anger, but they are not as good as British people at expressing fear or self-doubt. American athletes or soldiers are seldom quoted as admitting they are scared before combat. This contributes to the feeling of "bigness" in a wanderer nation, but both things stem from the basic human need to comfort those around us. If you are in a pioneering situation, then it is comforting to know that you are with tough, aggressive yet predictable people. But if you are in an over-crowded and well-ordered society it is far nicer to be with people who are gentle yet produce surprises. Thus in England, or Japan, one hides one's talents: the English piano maestro will only admit to "occasionally tinkling the ivories", while the Japanese will go further and insist that he is a very inferior player. When forced to try their host's piano they proceed to amaze with their virtuosity. This behaviour can seem very stupid and even deceitful to pioneering types, and a duality game builds up which suggests that we islanders are stuffy, repressed and small-minded compared to the "rambler-gamblers" of the new world.

My resolution of the wanderer/stay-at-home duality is the "dreamer". The dreamer can remain in bed, yet travel to the ends of the universe in space and time; he can also wander the whole world while thinking of nothing more than the home comforts he is missing. As with the Trickster in the Good/Bad duality, it is of course the dreamer who organises the whole wanderer/stay-at-home game: the magic of the wanderer lies in the dreams of those who stay at home, and the love and security of the stay-at-home is really a dream in the wanderer's mind as he waits at yet another dreary airport lounge.

That last example touches on another duality: romantic/classic. The charisma of the wanderer is a romantic quality, and classicism has a "stay at home" feel by comparison. More strictly the romantic impulse is to do with being swept away by emotions and greater cosmic forces like Nature with a capital N, whereas classicism is more concerned with careful structure and aesthetic laws. Nietzsche used the terms Dionysian and Apollonian to describe these two approaches to art: Dionysus was a god of intoxication, ecstacy and divine possession whereas

Apollo was a god of formal beauty and exquisite and har-monious proportions.

As with all vivid dualities we find the dance of paradox: for example the Zen or far Eastern approach to art which carries the classical approach to such extremes - one spends ages simply learning the exact way to hold one's brush or mix one's ink before you even make a mark on the paper - and yet whose end result is to achieve the greatest possible spontaneity.

I will opt for the terms Dionysian/Apollonian because they immediately suggest to me the third princi-ple should be Hermetic, after the god Hermes.

Appropriately enough, Hermes is the trickster fig-ure, the god of commerce and trickery as well as of com-munications and learning. So we can look at my solution on two levels.

On the "low brow" level the romantic/classic split is what makes artists wonder to what extent they should try to refine the principles and traditions they have learnt at art or music school, and to what extent they should chuck them all aside and "freely express themselves". To this dilemma Hermes' has a simple answer: "be commer-cial". Commercial art is utterly classical in its need to cal-culate and play by the market rules, and yet a major part of the calculation is to make the result look as romantic as possible - because it is romance that makes the cash tills ring.

On the "high brow" level, however, I see the Hermetic Tradition as a vital third force to Romanticism and Classicism: insofar as its method is so disciplined and cerebral it might seem to belong with Classicism, on the other hand its mystery and its invocation of great cosmic forces seems utterly Romantic. It is a genuine third way.

Each example poses a new problem. This time it is this: should I put this next example here or in the following subsection? Here I am still looking at "big" dualities in society because they are clearer and easier to resolve, this allows us to learn ways to recognise the third principle before tackling the difficult, personal inner dualities. The problem here considered is an outer one, but one that is fortunately not too big in society as a whole.

It concerns the duality of Fundamentalist Christianity versus the Occult or "Pagan" community. As part of the latter group, I have been very upset by the attacks made on us and their growing intensity in the last decade. Part of this is the anti-Satan hysteria: I have a tape of a fundamentalist fanatic listing among Satanic vices: "astrology, yoga, graphology, homeopathy and all Eastern Religions" amongst which he names Islam, Judaism and Communism (Karl Marx turns in his grave) but, surprisingly, not Christianity.

At times I have been quite incensed at these attacks and desirous of responding with all-out war on the bastards who do it in the name of a God of Love - but that is just the gut reaction of a dualistic fighter. The fact is that we occultists are a small and fragmented minority against the wealth and organisation of the various churches. All-out war would suit them very well. So how can I be true to mine own philosophy and find a third principle to de-fuse this battle?

The answer came during one council of war, when I realised our best ally was boring old Common Sense. When locked into the struggle, with my friends being hounded by the tabloids as "satanists", it seemed as if this struggle was a mighty battle which divided all of society into two camps - the spiritual explorers versus the spiritual tyrants or dogmatists. Detaching myself (like a worthy Trickster) I realised this was rubbish. We were both minorities: as far as the vast bulk of humanity is concerned, both fundamentalist christians and occultists are just whackoes on the fringe, both practicing a sort of mumbo jumbo magic that has no rational basis. There is nothing between us, just two groups of loonies at each other's throats.

This is one important lesson when seeking the third principle: it is sometimes really big, so much bigger than either side of the duality as to be almost invisible from within it. When trapped in dualistic battles, just look for the great "so what?".

So what was my suggestion to my fellow warriors in this council of war? It was just to keep firmly within common sense when under attack. See this as a debate before a vast audience: on stage the Occultist faces the Fundamentalist who accuses him of being involved with those who breed babies for ritual slaughter. There are now enormous temptations for the occultist to fight back in kind: to explain that witches and pagans revere life in all its forms; to point out the millions murdered in the name of christianity... Do that and the debate will become a public spectacle, a cock fight between two minority philosophies. Instead take the route of common sense and say that these tales of ritual murder sound most unsavoury and why is the accuser not pursuing the matter with the police rather than making a public performance about it? If there is evidence, should he not be acting immediately? If there is not, should he not be out there gathering it?

Forget all the self-righteous posturing of the wrongly accused - it will only confirm your own crankdom. Just treat the matter like the criminal matter it surely is and, in the eyes of the public, you are no longer the crank but the reasonable person faced with the loony. If you cannot see the Trickster in this role, just add a little gentle humour and you will have achieved it. Once you can laugh a little you will no longer be seen as an extremist, but a real person. That audience is on your side and the debate is laughed away.

Of our recent examples this is perhaps the neatest and cleanest because it is so sharply polarised. From within it is a real battlefield, from without a storm in a teacup despite its clear universal implications of tyranny versus freedom, good versus evil and all that. So this example could be the model for some of the nationalist battles in Eastern Europe, or the red-hot (at present) abortion debate in the USA. The public eventually grows tired of polemic and battles: the first group to successfully align with the great "so what?" of Common Sense will be the one to survive.

All the dualities considered so far have been long established biggies, and most have already been fed with the sacrificial blood of battle to make them yet more powerful. I would like to find a new duality that is still in the growing stage in case anything can be learnt from studying the way it takes hold.

My example is the "right brain, left brain" duality. I first came across this in the early seventies when someone called Ornstein was being quoted for his work on the two lobes of the human brain. The left lobe is linked to the right side of the body and usually specialises in linear thought processes such as spoken or written language, logic, causality and scheduling. The right lobe is linked to the left side of the body and usually specialises in multidimensional spatial thinking, bodily movement and pattern recognition processes.

Now a characteristic of the second type of thought is that it can seem instantaneous compared with linear thought: a picture or pattern is perceived as a whole in a flash, whereas a verbal argument or description must be listened through before it is taken in. So the idea of "intuition" is associated with the right brain. Combine that with the dancing and love-making aspects of bodily movement and the right brain begins to line up against the left brain along the old Play/Work duality with its attendant Fun/Boredom axis. An advertisement for Saab cars is published consisting of a two page spread. The left page says "a car for the left side of the brain" and consists of a description of the theory illustrated by the technical and safety features which make Saab the logical choice - a whole page of closely written facts and figures. The right page just shows the car swooping along in its glory with the heading "a car for the right side of the brain". Meanwhile the copy on the left contains the sentence "needs are boring; desires are what make life worth living" - in a context which links needs to the left brain and desires to the right brain.

Then another prejudice enters the duality. Sequential/Spatial becomes Logical/Illogical and is aligned with the familiar Masculine/Feminine duality. The left brain is labelled "masculine", the right brain "feminine" and both attract all the praise and condemnation that go with those labels. The next step is that the left/right theory becomes part of the battle of the sexes so that men are criticised for "left-brain nit-picking" and women for "right-brain woolliness".

This is where the paradoxical nature of duality is shown: for I understand that sex actually biases women toward left brain superiority over men. Everyone can be more or less developed either way (and left handedness can go with a reversal of the functions of the two lobes), however at puberty there is a tendency for women's left lobes to become better developed, while in men it is the right lobe that is inclined top predominate. It has been suggested that the primitive male needed the spatial sense of the right lobe when out hunting, while the woman needed language skills to manage the household; but whatever the reason the result shows as a bias in school-boys to prefer engineering subjects which require a strong spatial sense, while schoolgirls are a little more likely to opt for languages.

Going from statistical generality to the particular, I have noticed that my partner likes verbal directions to a location while I prefer a map of how to get there. Give me verbal instructions and I either forget them after the third instruction, or else I have unwittingly translated the instruction into a mental picture and I miss the turning because it does not "look" the way I had imagined. Once I have seen a map, however, I can demonstrate a quite uncanny sense of direction even after I've forgotten the actual detail of the map.

This difference has lead to disagreement, as has our different perception of time. Sometimes I am asked if I can do something the next day and I answer that I am too busy. Then I am asked to say what I am doing to make me so busy and I cannot give an answer that satisfies my partner. She wants me to list a full timetable so that she can work out why I do not have time to help; but I do not have a proper timetable and yet still know I have a full day ahead. To me a set of tasks is not so much a linear sequence of actions as a sort of box of bits which have to be shaken into place. If this is allowed to happen I can be very good at getting a lot done, laying me open to the criticism "you always manage to find time for your own work". But if I am asked to arrange a linear schedule so that a particular half hour can be left free, I'm not very good at it and my whole system seems to become ineffi-cient and bumbly. What's more, my inability to explain a clear schedule gives the impression that I am being eva-sive and trying to wriggle out of helping. Although this right brain spatial scheduling can be super-efficient at dovetailing tasks, left brain intervention can send it hay-wire.

Let us say it is a shopping trip: my partner might say that she wants to have a coffee now rather than after going to the ironmongers. To her linear schedule this is easy: take out the twenty minute coffee break from here and pop it into there. But to my spatial sense I am disrupted because in my world-view the coffee break involved a place as well as a time, and I am now somehow in the wrong place for my plan. A irritated sense of being "mucked about" arises in me and I have difficulty explaining why - because the right brain has to go to the left brain for this explanatory function.

I've expanded this a bit because really I'm dying to find out if other people of either sex have noticed a bias toward spatial and linear time and direction sense and whether it has got them into misunderstanding with those of the opposite persuasion.

Anyway, given that this is becoming a paradoxical and emotive duality, what about its resolution? What is the third factor? Faced with but two lobes we could have been in an irresolvable position, but my choice is that emotion itself is the third factor to the right/left brain duality. Emotion, I understand, originates not in either lobe but in the primitive limbic and reptilian part of the brain from which the two lobes sprout.

One promising sign is that this third factor has been claimed and disowned by both sides, just as liberalism has in right/left politics.

On the one hand you have a "left brain" logical stance which denies emotion and blames it on "the other" with all its "pre-verbal" nonsense - while the right brain dancer, sculptor or "man of action" jeers at left brain for being cold, analytical and unfeeling. In effect the Jungian Thinking/Feeling polarity has lined up with the left/right polarity and taken on the assumption that emotion is the same as feeling.

On the other hand you have the left brain claim that the only true expression of these feelings is via the left brain. To take a fully polarised model, imagine a couple where the woman is dissatisfied and expressing it in left brain language she nags and nags her husband until he takes right brain action and commits suicide. She goes to a counsellor and is told "don't feel guilty, honey, you just expressed your honest feelings and that is ok". But if the man had chosen instead to strangle the woman - expressing his honest feeling of distaste for this ill windpipe of venom by closing it forever - he would not be saluted for having expressed his feelings, but probably told that his brutal action was a consequence of not expressing them. A man can have a red face, bulging veins and clenched fists and yet be told he is not "expressing his anger". The assumption in many forms of counselling that the only expression of feelings is to be able to talk about them, whereas to a right-brain biassed person it might be much more of a release to go fishing, to lock oneself up in the workshop and plane some wood, to play the piano, slam a door or smash a plate, in fact to do almost any physical action except talk about the feeling. While to the left-brain all these physical actions amount to denials by someone who refuses to acknowledge their feelings - ie put them into words. The axes are now reversed: feeling has become a left brain matter.

So perhaps the polarity of left and right brain thinking can be rescued by the recognition that emotion is a third factor which can be expressed via either lobe in accordance with the feeler's own bias. And the awful pedantry among some groups of men might not be blamed so much upon the left brain as upon the fact that one works harder at areas where one is naturally less gifted. I gather that a group of businesswomen often reaches a sensible conclusion to negotiations in half the time it would take businessmen to do it.

In the next section I want to move from examining the big dualities of the outside world to the personal dualities within, and that, of course, could trip us up on another duality - that of Outer/Inner. So I must first suggest resolution of that.

The outer is the world of the extravert, the world of appearances and actions and objective facts and shared events. The inner is the subjective realm of thoughts and feelings and memories and impressions and all that is experienced when we turn our senses inwards to the mindscape.

Now this looks like a difficult duality to resolve, because it is surely like the directions North and South or the off/on of a switch - an unambiguous indication of objective difference. However we do find battles being fought or at least proposed over this divide: people who champion the "depth" of inner experience against the "shallowness" of outer appearance, and those who see the inner as "morbid introspection" while the outer is "healthy". So where there is battle I expect some hope of resolution.

Inner, outer... does that leave the surface which divides the two? No, because the surface is definitely the property of the outer with its "surface appearances". That approach is just an attempt to find a mean or midway position.

Try instead to consider the cyclic effects of a trinity. Whereas the journey from one end of a duality to the other leaves us no option but to turn back and reverse the journey, with a trinity one can go beyond that end point and progress round to the third point as in my examples of Fritz and of politics.

Those who turn from the outer world to the inner, what do they aspire to? Those who take their inner experience and project it out onto the world, what do they arrive at? Is not the answer "the spirit"?

The spirit which is neither inner nor outer yet permeates both. The inner search leads to spirit, as long as the hermit progresses in meditation beyond the confines of navel-gazing. And having found it he is in a position like Zarathustra to return to the outer world and preach, thus continuing the cycle. Looking out at the world after an inner search we see a spirit behind things (even if only the spirit of physical law) and we can learn enough of it to come to understand our own inner states - and thus continue the cycle.

That last example suggests to me a particular application of the inner/outer duality based upon the direction of movement or flow. The other day I scraped the skin of my feet and noticed the bare patches weeping pus. Assuming that nothing was as healthy as fresh air I left the wound uncovered, and it kept on weeping for days with increasing discomfort. So I discovered an old box of what is called "Second Skin" dressing: a sort of damp gel that is laid on the wound, to keep it moist, then covered with elastoplast. Reckoning that the wound kept running - even more in the sunshine - because my body actually wanted it to be wet, I decided to try this wet approach. It was not natural to me - to whom air and fire were the healers and water a distinctly dank and festering element.

On the box it recommended changing the dressing every 8 hours or so, so I asked a nurse about this and she said no, I should leave it on for days and days even if it looks horribly grungy underneath. She said there was a new concept in wound treatment: no longer all the emphasis on cleaning up, drying with lint and letting the wound "breath": the latest technique for burns was to cover the skin with plastic and leave the body's own smelly processes to work themselves out.

These reversals in medical practice tickle me. As a child I was told to use sticky plaster for every wound; as a young adult I learnt to let things breath and nature would heal, now I am told to cover up and heal myself. Broken limbs were once set in plaster for ages; now I gather that there is a strong emphasis on using the limb as soon as possible.

I suppose it is the reinstatement of water as healer in place of air that intrigues me. In place of a laying things open you close them in and let them work under cover. These abrupt swings of fashion in medicine suggest to me that they reflect not the careful, step by step accretion of medical understanding so much as the play of cosmic forces. (Well, I would feel that as an intuitive, fiery type I suppose.)

Water pushes Air off the healer's throne. It could have interesting repercussions on the business of therapy and counselling.

At present there is much emphasis on laying it all open, of "airing" matters and not keeping anything bottled up. The direction is all outward - if you have a feeling, then express it for healing. I like the theory of that, it is like my instinct to expose my wound to the air and sunshine. It is a choleric formula often preached by those angry souls who need to express their anger at others and argue that this is healthy and proper compared to those who do not do this and who, they deduce, must be holding back their anger.

But I am also aware of a melancholic formula. If I am feeling bad it would be a sham, a trick or a positive effort for me to work up some anger and express it outwardly. I usually fall instead into a sort of sadness. This state looks and feels awfully like depression, and yet there is a difference. With the passing of time I have learnt that melancholy is not as harmful as depression, all it wants is to be left alone to work itself out. Typically, for a small melancholy, a good night's sleep after an evening on my own will allow me to awake fresh and full of hope the next day. I have learnt to see my melancholy as something like a gentle warm bath that heals inner hurts and wounds. Just the sort of thing I need after a choleric person has unleashed their anger on me. So threatening do I find choleric outbursts that it took me many years to realise that cholerics find melancholy equally threatening: they see rejection in my need to be left alone, they see accusation in the sadness and sighing.

This then shows a polarity of healing methods: an outward directed approach where everything must be expressed "honestly" and nothing held back, and an inner approach where the wounds are covered over and left to gently digest. Now certain peoples champion the first approach and see the other as distinctly unhealthy. For example, the New Age Californian who would have all feelings expressed outright and who is utterly opposed to the English or Japanese inclination towards reserve and inner solutions. Such a person would be able to trace all the ills of British society to the "repression of feelings". And yet, if we ask which societies are the most healthy and un-neurotic, my impression is that the outer expression of feeling has not solved absolutely everything. Some Americans that I meet in the lounges of Cotswold hotels would even give the impression that our twisted, repressed British way of life has a certain soothing charm.

So I wonder if the pendulum will swing in the inner world of psychological healing as it has in the outer world of physical healing? Are we about to see a new school of counselling based upon constructive melancholia, where we are allowed to feel sadness, shame, loneliness, failure and such emotionsthat have been banished by the positive-thinking school? Might not the "inner workshop" of the late nineties consist of people sitting brooding in corners instead of thumping cushions all together in a circle?

The relevance is this. Duality as explained by me is a combative, choleric influence which leads us to project our fears and fight them in outsiders. Trinity takes a more watery and alchemic approach in that it tells us to seek a third principle or solution which will make the duality flow - that is, dissolve it. This solution is allowed to flow in its container, a primal unity behind the trinity and my intention is that some final precipitate or benefit will eventually accrue.

Trinity is the closed wound, allowed to heal itself with its own natural process: for the Mercurial third principle was always there, just waiting to be discovered and allowed to work.

Turn inward with a sharp eye. Close the vessel. Let its contents ferment. Keep your sword out of it, yet sharp and ready for the opening of the egg.

Now for the individual.

THE TRINITY AS PSYCHOLOGICAL PROCESS

After the build up in the last bit, this could be something of an anti-climax, because I can do no more than extend a personal example and leave you to find your own solutions.

The object of the last part was to run through lots of outer examples of dualities which find their resolution, in the hope that a feeling for the process is gained by induction, and that certain signs will come to be recognised and looked for. There is also the hope that, among the more or less light-hearted descriptions, there will be one or more which cause a jolt of recognition, a sense of an inner truth laid bare or an old dilemma shifted. If every one of my examples fell away like water off a duck's back, then this section will have little more to add.

In the "outer" I went forth looking for dualities like a hunter, poking in bushes and lifting stones to unearth all sorts of prey. I don't particularly suggest that you go looking for your inner dualities in this way: as long as they are not troubling you, why bother? The intention now is rather to cope with real problems that arise of their own accord.

Yesterday there were two items on the news that upset me. In one a young mother had been raped and killed in a London park while walking her dog. Her battered and muddy two year old son was found hugging her dead body and in a state beyond speech. In the other a gang of joyriders near Swindon had opened the gate to a field and used the car to chase and terrify a herd of cows, leaving two of them severely wounded and in pain so that they had to be destroyed.

The second story made me very angry, the first very sad. The image of a little muddy thekker clinging to its dead mother in a park made me weep. I was not aware of great anger, though I would have surely dealt harshly with the attacker had I witnessed the event. Somehow the tragedy was too great for me to take on anger: I almost felt sad for the attacker who could do such a thing.

But I was not aware of much sadness about the cows, just blazing anger. This is the clue to my problem. You might say that I have a perfect right to be angry at such an act, and a good job too, but the point is that I was *too* angry. Mentally I caught the gang and enacted such vicious acts of revenge on them as would make readers' hair curl were I to spell them out. What I wanted to do to *them* would make *their* treatment of the cows seem like a mere rib-ticklin' jape. Their entrails would have stretched for miles across the country.

I recognised this rage in me as an old pattern of rage against the thug, bully or yob. The farmer interviewed spoke of the "mindlessness" of their act and I would say he is close to the point, but my general lack of charity in this direction means that I would first like to examine the word closely in case any hint of positivity is retained by it. I would not, for example, wish by this usage to commend the gang as exemplars of the Zen doctrine of no-mind.

At times in my life I have seen something like a vandalised tree or flower bed and felt this surge of almost intoxicating rage. At other times it has been tales of brutality or torture that have fired me. In each case my reaction has been a desire to return the violence one zillion-fold: so no claims here to my being a servant of the light against the powers of darkness.

What is it that makes me so angry? I long ago realised that only some inner duality could have such power to rend my soul. It is something like the bully and the victim, and something like the gentleman and the thug. Were it just the bully and the victim, I would surely have been enraged instead of saddened by the woman's death. There is something in the mindlessness idea. It is not so much the intensity of sadism as the callous non-recognition of the others' pain. One assumes the gang went away laughing and slept soundly that night after a good bout of sex. One assumes this quite arbitrarily: for they may have been insensibly drunk, they could have been working off sexual frustration taking the cow as symbol, perhaps they were even arguing with the driver who was acting out of defiance to his friends' admonitions not to be so bloody daft. All these and more are possible, yet my anger focusses on the image of that jeering, carefree mob who are out for laughs at any expense.

The shadow of my beloved Trickster, maybe? A funny man in bovver boots, detached, cynical, amused by the fury engendered by his actions and not giving a tuppeny fuck for the consequences. Crack another tin of lager and lob the container into the stream. Litter lout.

The other week I was walking in Stroud's Stratford park and seeing lots of litter scattered about. Blood began to simmer. Then a Pepsi cup landed on my head from a high tree. There was a squirrel; there were the torn open dustbin bags and the many trails of litter from those bags to the trees. Nature: the ultimate litter lout. Bark-stripping squirrels: the ultimate yobs. And yet it seemed more tiresome and amusing than enraging. Here was a lower order of mindlessness than any gang, and yet it did not seem to matter so much. It is not the *actual act* so much as a *sense of something in the mind of the perpetrators* that bothers me.

With Venus well aspected in my fourth house I have often lived in the sort of beautiful surroundings that challenge the yob. I was living and teaching at Eton in the days before the Windsor bridge was closed, when it formed the highway between the slums of Slough and the nightlife of Windsor, and all manner of rollicking crowds walked through in the evening yelling or revving noisy motorbikes. All this was very tiresome to a resident, and yet I sort of understood the urge to make a little extra noise simply because Eton is what it is; the urge to talk dirty just that bit louder in the hope of making the net curtains twitch disapprovingly. One night a party of us masters were in London when our car's exhaust pipe fell off. We were, of course, gentlemen enough not to relish the ear-splitting roar of an unsilenced engine under full throttle, and we made our way back as peaceably as we could... until we reached Eton High Street. At that point the master at the wheel put his foot down to the floor and made the very windows rattle as we burned up the street. I have seldom laughed so much in my life, I was aching and nearly sick. We were feeling exactly the pleasure that the yobs got as they raped the peace of Eton, but we knew it so much more poignantly for the fact that we were respected masters of the very institution itself.

That was when I realised how the yob and the gent are so closely intertwined. Hard-liners note that liberal societies harbour the worst yobs, and they assume that the wishy washiness of liberalism somehow allows a natural yob tendency to break out. I do not think so. Those squirrels had the action of a yob, but with none of the cachet. I do not believe that it is the weakness of liberalism that permits the yob, but rather it is the decency of liberalism that evokes him. Gentlemanly behaviour offers more than mere social respect, as I explained under the snobbery bit above, it has distinct sensual advantages that make the yob a very sorry comparison. But the one overwhelming pleasure of yobbery is that of being un-gentle, and of visualising the horror of the genteel.

It was years later that I realised the real yob in myself - not just the occasional yob. I realised that I am an ideas yob. Show me a set of neat and tidy assumptions and I want to trample all over it - just like the vandaliser of a flower bed. If someone says "of course the country is in a sorry state with all those immigrants", or "no wonder AIDS is rampant after all that 60s permissiveness", or "nothing will get better till the patriarchy is overthrown" or whatever... then I have an enormous urge to overturn those assumptions, rip up the flower beds, smash the windows and puke over this tidy philosophy. It is the "of courses" and the "no wonders" that make me want to do it, the theories themselves hardly concern me. "Of course" around a prejudice is to me what a neat box hedge around a Park's Department flower bed is to the vandal.

It is all very well for me to argue that my yobbery doesn't do any actual physical harm, that is simply to claim that outer security matters more than inner security. The fact is that there is a yob in me, and that is my response to primness and pedantry.

Another of my lovely living places was in a town mill overlooking the river Itchin in the ancient city of Winchester. There I could look down on beautifully tended flower beds, crystal clear waters and families of ducks, swans and moorhens. Here again the yobs' voices would rise a decibel or two as they made their way home on Summer nights as the pubs closed. One evening I watched two young men pelting a family of ducklings with stones - not just the odd stone but a continuing game. I felt anger. I could easily just have seethed and done nothing, or I could at least in theory have expressed it by slaughtering those two. Actually I simply went down the stairs and out and walked past them and back with a sort of bristling, ominous intensity. I said "good evening" as I passed and they looked a bit sheepish. They went home. I had neither repressed my anger, nor sublimated it by calling the police or writing to the paper, but somehow "owned" it. I felt fine, and the ducklings were no longer being tormented.

So there is something bubbling in me. Many strange things are sweating in that vessel. I understand why it is particularly the liberal papers like the Guardian and the Observer who are fascinated by exposes of thuggery: cock-fighting in the shires, bare-fist fighting in sweaty city basements. On the other hand when I see the tabloids try that game with their monotonously recycled announcements of "a new level of mindless thuggery sweeping through our young" backed by quotations from kids saying things like "who cares who suffers, we just want a fucking good laugh" then I can laugh out loud: what kid wouldn't say something like that just for the fun of the reaction? Also in the vessel is my fascination with the phenomenon of "survivalism" and memories of letters to the pages of survival and weaponry magazines in which the writers slagged off the press for persecuting the survival movement, then went on to make the highly political statement that there is nothing political about survivalism. I have pondered the mentality of politicians who describe vicious acts as "unthinkable" - have they so little imagination? Is there really no part of them that would yearn for the joy of machine gunning a gang of yobs to death or bulldozing their bodies into a mass grave?

Part of me would obtain immense aesthetic pleasure from emptying a few belts of machine gun ammo into a coach load of hooligans. That part has a loud voice, yet it is not overpowering. It is just one of many loud voices, another of which would condemn such acts as not very nice.

Come off it! Shut up! Get on with it! Stop this waffle, were dying for the answer! You've given us the yob and the gent duality - ok then, what's the solution this time?

Aha. The vessel is closed my friends. This is not the section about easy answers to society's problems, this is about sorting one's own inner hell. It is my facility with the former that gives me hope for the latter. My vessel is closed, it is sweating and I watch it carefully like an alchemist's alembic. Sometimes there are clouds within, sometimes bolts of lightning, and sometimes beautiful colours. A process is continuing and it sometimes hurts but, when I see what is happening elsewhere in the world, I realise this is true healing. The third principle is there, I know it but cannot yet name it. Maybe the Great Work will generate that Philosopher's Stone to heal all liberal nightmares.

Leave me to brood - this is my business. I have indicated a path - that is now your business.

STALKING THE WILD TRINITY

This is the section that should expand to half the book if it were hoping to find a place on the occult shelves of the High Street book store. But I go on holiday tomorrow and I had a sort of pact with myself that I would consider committing suicide if the book was not finished by then.

This section is about all those little avenues of exploration taken by me over my years of seeking to penetrate to the essence of trinity.

In order to get a feel for the Tetrahedron of Elements described in the previous part, I made one out of brightly coloured Fymo and gleaming aluminium rods. Spheres of Fymo - stuff on sale in hobby shops, it moulds like plasticine but sets hard on baking - coloured red for Fire, yellow for Air, green for Earth and blue for Water. I chose the fluorescent type of Fymo and it looked weird under ultra-violet light, glowing in the dark.

I found a tetrahedral variant on the Rubik cube called the "Pyraminx". Having fewer combinations it was easier to solve than the cube and more seductive for casual manipulation. Its faces are coloured red, green, blue and yellow and I can align it so that each face faces to the correct quarter on the traditional scheme: blue to the West, red to the South, green to the North and yellow to the East. Manipulating it gives a sense of tetrahedral form, and the shape is divided along each side into three so that each face has 3x3 or 9 triangles.

My pursuit of trinities took me to Sir Thomas Tresham's Triangular Lodge at Rushton in Northamptonshire where I meditated on AUM. This lodge is a hymn to the Holy Trinity made in brick and stone. It has three sides, each 33 feet long and three storeys; there are three gables on each side and a total of nine gargoyles. The walls are littered with trefoil forms in threes and the central chimney is three sided. The windows are triangular and divide like my Pyraminx into nine sub-triangles. The building is full of ciphers and magical symbols, including three latin inscriptions of 33 letters.

I was happy to discover a wealth of trinities incorporated in another holy building by a catholic fanatic: Woodchester Park near Stroud is a far more practical edifice but full of mystery in that it was never completed.

Among my objects of meditation was a tetrahedron of rock crystal purchased at a New Age festival from folk who had a thing about a great tetrahedron of power whose equilateral base spanned Glastonbury, Old Winchester Hill in Hampshire and somewhere near Stow on the Wold. The crystal tetrahedron has its points bevelled flat for structural strength and when you look into each face this presents the inner reflected form of a perfect icosahedron - Figure 6. Deep mysteries for those who have ears to hear, from someone who no longer has time to spell (or even work) them out.

My collection of triune forms includes mysterious agate triangles, and a sphere of rutilated quartz which exhibits a three-branch star like the Mercedes symbol when held to a bright light. One or two rutile spheres I have seen show this structure.

There is a set of tapes available called "Shape Tapes" where the sounds are generated from shapes. I have failed my readers by not getting the triangle tape and blasting my mind with it.

On the other hand I have built a mighty tetrahedron of six six foot (or two metre) canes and passed long hours seated within it and meditating upon these mysteries. A variation on pyramid power where the pure essence of the tetrahedron is used as a "power form" rather than the mixed symbolism of the pyramid which comprises four triangles and one square base.

The centre of gravity of such a tetrahedron lies three quarters of the way from its uppermost point down to the base. Now the height of a tetrahedron is approximately point eight or four-fifths of the length of one side (eg a tetrahedron of one metre sides would be about eighty centimetres high) and so the centre of gravity lies about one fifth of a side length above the base (eg twenty centimetres above the base of a pyramid of side one metre) – Figure 7.

NOTE
Figures 6 and 8 are photos not included in this edition

So when seated in the centre of my tetrahedron made of six foot canes, this power focus is just about fourteen inches above the ground. When kneeling in the "thunderbolt" posture at the centre of this structure my navel is approximately at the centre of power; if I sit cross legged then it is my solar plexus which is at the centre - Figure 8. This is useful when using the tetrahedron as a meditation structure: one can visualize it focusing its energies (to use the New Age lingo) into the appropriate part of the

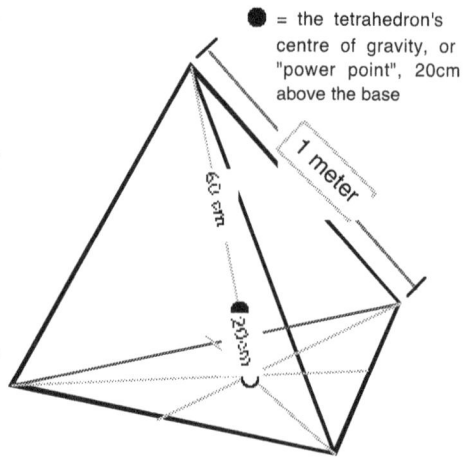

● = the tetrahedron's centre of gravity, or "power point", 20cm above the base

1 meter

60 cm

20 cm

Figure 7

A tetrahedron of 1 metre side, showing the position of its "power point". In a tetrahedron of side six feet, this point would be about 14 inches above the middle of the base

body. Another technique is to focus those energies into some object which can serve as a talisman: for example, a crystal or vial of spring water suspended on a string just about three-quarters of the height in length will be just at this point of power and will receive the full energy. So if I set up my tetrahedron of six foot canes and hang a small bottle of spring water from the top of the structure on a string about fifty eight inches long, then the bottle will in theory begin to charge up with tetrahedron energies - whatever that means. These practices will be expanded in the following section.

Deep mysteries have fanned the embers of my soul within this structure and the torch of knowledge has been lit like some Olympic flame from those sparks and carried over these years to inflame my writing herein.

It lies within the reader's power to make these fragments cosmic.

YE YCLEPT KEY TO YE TRINITARIAN ARCANA OF HIGH MAGICK

In this section I will assume some familiarity with magic of the Western Mystery tradition. The idea is not so much to provide everyone with a complete system of magic from square one, as to suggest to those already familiar with magical practice ways in which their practices can be adapted to the tetrahedral pattern of elements.

But to save this section from being totally worthless to others, I will begin with a bare bones description of how magic is done. It begins with some intention on the part of the magician: this can be anything from a desire to heal to a desire to avenge, from a desire to gain something to a desire to give thanks for something that already is. This desire is then expressed or enacted in a symbolic "language" within a symbolic framework - and the theory is that it will induce something like the desired result in the so-called "real" world.

I start with a very familiar example, even though it is one seldom practiced by serious modern magicians: sticking pins in a wax effigy of an enemy is a notorious technique for causing him harm. Here the intention is to hurt; the symbolic structure is a wax model of the person, and the symbolic language is that a pin piercing that structure represents a wound or disease to the victim. Another example is of the New Ager who begins the day writing down the affirmation "I love myself and feel boundless confidence". Here the intention is to gain confidence, the symbolic structure is a pen and paper and the language is English.

Such techniques require a certain level of belief to work. So you need a theory or model to justify them, and there are a choice of theories that have been mapped by Pete Carroll in "Psychonaut".

One type of theory assumes spiritual intervention. In the case of the wax doll, you might believe that this wicked act attracts demons who then go to your enemy and deliver your revenge upon him. In the case of the affirmation you might believe that the act of writing it attracts Angels of Love and Confidence who then inspire your being and heal your insecurities.

Another type of theory assumes an energy model: sticking in those pins expresses your anger and creates a sort of thunderbolt of angry energy which seeks release in the victim's body. The affirmation can be said to "raise one's energies" or make them "more positive", and if you believe that you are half way there. Note that occultists use the word energy in a particular way different to the scientific notion of a scalar quantity.

Another type of theory uses an information model. The physical act of sticking in pins imprints the desire to hurt into the information structure of the universe (like keying it into a computer console) and it will find its way through the software of existence to the victim's life-program. Similarly, the affirmation "keys" the desire into the unconscious mind, and so makes it become real.

Magical practice allows one to assume whatever theory is most appropriate and effective. The only rule seems to be that the harder the theory is to believe, the more dramatic the results will be if you do manage to believe it. It is easy to believe that an affirmation simply informs the unconscious mind, and that produces reasonable results. If, however, you really are able to convince yourself that it "raises positive energies" or whatever, the results will be far better. And if you can go the whole hog and imagine all those hoards of angels clustering round to help you... then you are a better man than me.

So that is the three-fold basis of the sort of magic I am dealing with: an intention, a structure, and a symbolic language.

Now the point is that a vast majority of formal magic has for a long time been based on a four-fold, cruciform structure called the cross of the elements or, in the Red Indian tradition, the Medicine Wheel. The magician stands in a circle with the element Air to the East, Fire to the South, Water to the West and Earth to the North. Appropriate colours, objects and sayings are then made to those four quarters to reinforce this symbolic structure. Then within this structure the symbolic magical acts are performed.

My suggestion is that this two-dimensional cross should be replaced by a three-dimensional tetrahedron. I also suggest that the system be linked to tradition by keeping the same symbolic structure of elements and attributes and merely adapting it slightly to reflect new ways of working.

The basis for this change has been explained at the end of the previous part: ask why the four quarters are chosen and the normal reply will be that "the Sun rises in the East, is highest in the South, sets in the West and is at its nadir in the North". But, as I explained, this is only true on two days a year, namely at the Equinoxes. It is true that the Sun rises in the East at the Spring Equinox, and it sets in the West, but from then on it proceeds to rise earlier and earlier and more and more towards the North East each day until Midsummer. Similarly it sets more and more toward the North West as we progress toward Midsummer.

So I argue that all those Summertime rituals performed out of doors should really be performed in a triangle: one point lies where the Sun rises, another where it is at noon, and the third where it sets. There is no fourth point because we do not see the Sun at midnight.

This scheme sounds symbolically better, but it would require prior research every time to determine exactly where the Sun rises and sets - noon is no problem as that lies to the South all the time. So what if we simplified matters and simply standardised on an equilateral triangle with one point facing South? Standing at the centre of that triangle we would find that its three points were at bearings of 60, 180 and 300 degrees - Figure 9. Now I note that the famous "Michael" ley line running across England (according to "The Sun and The Serpent" by Broadhurst and Miller) makes a bearing of 60 degrees to North, and this is claimed to be the direction of sunrise at Beltane and Lammas. According to the above text *"Beltane (May Day) and Llughnasad (Lammas) were the high spots of the ancient world... around which the whole year revolved...".* As Beltane marks the half way between the Spring Equinox and Midsummer, and Lammas marks the half way between Midsummer and the Autumn Equinox, and as an English magician standing in my equilateral triangle on those days would see the Sun rise over the Air (sunrise) point, be at its highest over the fire (noon) point, and set over the Water (sunset) point, it therefore seems that this triangle would be a very suitable shape to use for all Summer magic in England at least (and, in keeping with the trendy nationalistic fervour

Figure 9

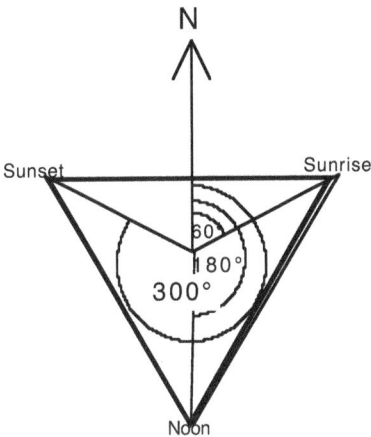

Bearings from a centre point

now sweeping the world, "bugger the others"). Assuming a certain symmetry, we would then use a similar triangle with its point to the North for Winter night-magic: because around Halloween and Candlemass (the other two fire festivals) the Sun would set over the Water (sunset) point, reach its invisible nadir at the Northern Earth point, and rise at the Air (sunrise) point.

Using these two triangular structures we now apply the traditional attributions summarised as follows:

Sunrise point. This corresponds to the element Air, the Angel Raphael and the magician's Intellect or Thinking function. The Dagger or Sword belongs at this point because its sharp blade symbolises the analytical function of thought and its role in banishing rituals corresponds to the intellectual ability to "explain away" spiritual phenomena. A fan or feather is another object that can be placed here to symbolise Air. If Fire is represented in the South by an actual candle flame, then incense could go here because it is seen as smoke (otherwise we tend to associate incense with Fire). The colour is yellow or orange.

Noon point. This corresponds to the element Fire, the Angel Michael and the magician's Will, Imagination or Intuitive function. The Wand belongs at this point as a director of energies or intentions (eg the pencil as Wand, used to write one's intention). A lamp, candle or charcoal censer for burning incense also belongs here because they represent Fire. The colour is bright red.

Sunset point. This corresponds to the element Water, the angel Gabriel and the magician's Emotions or Feeling function. The Cup or Bowl belongs at this point and represents acceptance, an ability to listen (the cupped ear) and a container in which transformation takes place. The colour is blue or turquoise green.

Midnight point. This corresponds to the element Earth, the angel Uriel and the magician's wealth, Physical body or Sensation function. The Disk belongs here, as would coins or tokens of wealth. The colour is dark green, brown or black.

So far I have talked in terms of the base triangle. Rather than omit the fourth element, it is placed at the fourth point of the tetrahedron - ie above the centre of the triangle. The appropriate instrument can either be hung at this point, or else it can be placed at the centre of the triangle to represent that fourth point. This means that the fourth element - far from being banished - plays a special presiding role in this new structure.

In the case of Summer or Day magic, Earth is the fourth element because there is no point to the North. So the Disk would either hang above the magician's head, or else be placed at the centre of the triangle to play an active part in the ritual. In the case of Winter night magic it is Fire or the Wand which either hangs over the magician's head or stands at the centre.

This new position for the fourth element suggests the need to adapt the traditional symbols to meet their new role.

Consider the Disk. In traditional usage this is a fairly passive instrument: usually just a symbolic disk that is placed to the North, though it might become a round loaf in more folksy traditions or a plate to hand round drinks and food. If the Disk is now going to play a central role it needs to be more useful: a round loaf, a plate or tray would be a good symbol in rituals where nourishment is to be handed out. Otherwise I suggest that a flat drum or gong makes a better Disk. When the intention is to work in a silent, meditative manner, then a gong could be suspended over the magician's head and struck to mark the beginning of the meditation: as its sound slowly fades the magician focusses into the growing silence. When the intention is to perform a dynamic ritual, the drum is a useful instrument to represent Earth. One of the requirements of the Disk was that it should have a symbol for the macrocosm inscribed on it: in the case of the Drum this means drawing a symbolic map such as the Tree of Life or Zodiac circle. This pattern will define its own magical operations: you strike the Drum at a certain sequence of points on the map, and that defines a rhythm for that operation.

In Winter/Night magic it is the Wand or Fire that stands at the fourth point. When the intention is to meditate quietly it is obviously appropriate just to hang a lamp above the magician's head to represent Fire. For more active magic I suggest that an appropriate form of Wand would be the classic conjurer's wand, or better still a torch or laser beam for tracing sigils in the dark of Winter. Again, I will describe these later.

Now the existence of a dyad of Summer and Winter magics ruled by Earth and Fire does raise the question of two more types of magic, perhaps oriented East and West, where the presiding elements would presumably be Water and Air. The difficulty here is that a triangle with one point to the East is not so simply understood: its points represent one sunrise and two sunsets, ie East is the Equinox sunrise and the other two points aline with Summer and Winter sunsets. No obvious meaning stems from this fact, so let us instead consider the fact that Water would be the fourth or presiding element. Here we would want the Cup to play a dynamic role and so it would be appropriate either to have a Bowl and be mixing some potion or elixir in it, or else to use a Tibetan-style "singing bowl" and be meditating with it.

Again, for the West-oriented magic, the element of Air presides and I would suggest that the Dagger be used to carve a fetish or talisman.

Because these last two structures are not so obvious, I suggest that they be considered as "advanced magic" and not used until the Summer and Winter magics have been well established.

Before explaining how to establish these structures, I need to say something about the symbolic languages to be used in them.

Basically, we take over all the traditional symbolic language from the old cruciform magic. When you would have chanted, you chant; when you would have danced, you dance; when you would have burned incense, you burn incense; when you would have meditated, you meditate; and so on.

But there is a need for a new or adapted ritual of banishment and invocation, because the traditional pentagram ritual is highly cruciform in nature and does not lend itself to a tetrahedral structure (not only does it refer to the four quarters, it also recognises the vertical axis, thus blowing the chance of chucking one element overhead).

I chose to adapt the far less often used hexagram ritual. I suspect that the reason that it is so seldom used is because it does not really belong in the old cruciform tradition: the ritual is very trinitarian in pattern and I find far more satisfactory when adapted to the tetrahedral structure. True, the opening chant "I N R I" does contain four letters, but the first and the last are the same and so bring one back to the beginning just as one might trace the three sides of a triangle and end up at the first point - Figure 10.

The use of the Drum as Disk suggests a new symbolic language based on the rhythmic beating of symbols drawn on the drum skin - an exciting addition to the magical repertoire mentioned above. If, for example, you had the symbols of the planets on your Drum, then an operation to increase wealth could use the rhythm "Venus - Jupiter, Jupiter - Venus" (2 beats on Jupiter as invocation, sandwiched between single beats on Venus to indicate area of influence).

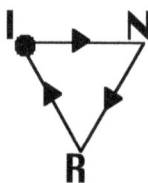

Figure 10
INRI as a
three-letter
word

ESTABLISHING THE NEW MAGIC

I suggest that this is done over a period of a year to allow time to make the necessary instruments, explore the symbolism and adjust to the change. The magician should already be fully familiar with the traditional magic based on the four quarters and he or she should already have a Wand, Dagger or Sword, Cup and Disk and know how to perform the lesser Pentagram ritual.

You will be establishing a tetrahedron as a working space. For the solo worker it is convenient to make this just as tall as you can reach with your Dagger. Then divide that height by 0.8 to see how long the six sides of your tetrahedron will be. I can just about reach 96 inches and so, dividing by 0.8 (ie dividing by four and multiplying by five) I get 120 inches or ten feet as the side of my tetrahedron. The Pythagorean number of perfection - nice one, Philotunus. It would help visualisation if six canes were obtained and erected into a tetrahedron and the work done initially within this structure until it can be easily visualised. For larger sizes, white ribbon can be used to mark the six edges, as long as there is some overhead point to attach the three sloping edges to.

The altar should be just one quarter of the height - in this case 24 inches - in order that its top should be at the centre of the tetrahedron when placed in the middle of the triangle - Figure 11. A triangular top is rather awkward so I suggest a hexagonal (six sided) top to the altar lined up nicely with the base of the tetrahedron - Figure 12.

The operation begins at Beltane, ie the day when Sun arrives at fifteen degrees Taurus (5-8th May). The temple has been prepared with a tetrahedron in place, lined up with one point facing South for Summer magic. In the centre of the tetrahedron stands the altar and on it are his four magical weapons: Dagger, Disk, Cup and Wand. The magician enters the temple before dawn and performs the traditional lesser banishing ritual of the pentagram then sits in silence until the Sun rises. As the Sun rises he declares "It is my (our) will to establish the structure for Summer Day magic". The magician then takes the Dagger and uses it

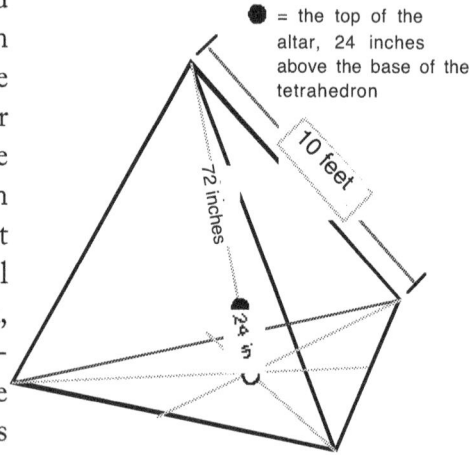

● = the top of the altar, 24 inches above the base of the tetrahedron

72 inches

10 feet

24 in

Figure 11. My working tetrahedron 96 inches high

to define the edges of the tetrahedron: the shape is not unicursal, so the correct procedure is to begin with the point overhead then draw it down to the Sunrise point; return overhead then draw it down to the Noon point; return overhead then draw down to the Sunset point; from their the point is drawn along to the Sunrise point, down to the Noon point and back to the Sunset

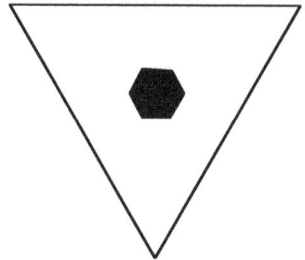

Figure 12

Suggested hexagonal altar, aligned with sides of base triangle

point, thus tracing the triangular base of the tetrahedron - Figure 13. This act is equivalent to the statement "I use my analytical ability to define this structure or universe of operation": you may, if you wish, repeat those words as you mark out the tetrahedron with the dagger.

The dagger is now placed at the Sunrise point, the Wand at the Noon point and the Cup at the Sunset point; the Disk remains on the altar or is ideally hung overhead at the top point. You can also light incense and place it at the first or second point as appropriate, you can place a lighted candle at the second point and you can put wine or water into the Cup. Then I suggest you sit and meditate beside the altar. End with the normal pentagram banishing ritual and put back the instruments.

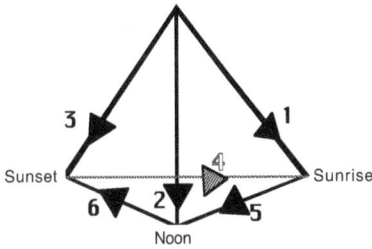

Figure 13. Sequence for defining the space.

Between Beltane and midsummer you have about six weeks in which to repeat this practice. It is not necessary to do it just at sunrise now - any time between sunrise and sunset is ok. The second job is to practice the movements of the hexagram ritual in preparation for Midsummer. Your third task is to make a lamp and wand (see later description) for consecration at Midsummer.

Before noon on the day the Sun enters Cancer (Midsummer) you should enter the temple prepared as before but the old Wand is no longer placed on the altar, instead you bring in your new Wand and lamp which are placed on the altar. You begin as before with the pentagram but this time the statement of intent is "It is my will to consecrate the new Wand and Lamp". At noon the tetrahedron is marked and the usual actions performed. This time the new Wand and Lamp are placed in the noon point with the words "with this act I consecrate this Wand and Lamp to the New Magic". You then sit and meditate as before but paying particular attention to the symbolism of the new Wand and Lamp. When finished, you no longer use the pentagram banishing ritual, instead you take your new Wand and perform the hexagram banishing ritual.

Between midsummer and Lammas you continue to practice as before, but now you always use the new wand and the only banishing ritual performed is the hexagram ritual to open and close.

At Llughnasad or Lammas (ie on the day the Sun enters fifteen degrees Leo, 2-7th August) you again perform a sunrise ritual as at Beltane. This time the affirmation changes to "It is my (our) will to confirm the structure for Summer Day magic" (as opposed to "establish" the structure). You now have about six weeks to obtain or construct a new Cup to dedicate to the new magic. I suggest obtaining a singing bowl and decorating it with symbols of your choice.

At the Autumn equinox you enter the temple a little before sunset. This time the old cup is not on the altar but you carry in your new Cup and place it there. The statement of intent is now "It is my (our) will to consecrate this Cup to the New Magic". The ritual is performed as before and this time the new cup is placed to the sunset point with the words "with this act I consecrate this Cup to the New Magic". You pour some spring water or wine into the cup before meditating on it as you did on the Wand and Lamp at midsummer. If it is a singing bowl, put just a little liquid in it so that you can still sound the bowl. After the meditation drink most of the liquid except for a little which is poured onto the earth (if outside) or used to anoint the altar as an offering. End with the hexagram banishing as before.

Between now and Samhain no magic is performed this year, though one can simply sit in the tetrahedron and meditate at odd times during the day.

At Samhain (as Sun enters 15 degrees Scorpio, 5-7 November) the Winter magic is inaugurated. Begin just before Sunset with a temple prepared with the tetrahedron with one point facing North. On the altar there is your old Dagger and Disk, and the new Cup, Wand and Lamp. The initial banishing for this once is according to the old pentagram ritual. The statement is "It is my (our) will to establish the structure for Winter Night magic". As the sun sets this is said and you trace out the tetrahedron with the dagger in its new orientation (beginning from on high, trace down to the Sunset point, then the Midnight point, then the Sunrise point; then trace a triangle - Sunset, Midnight, Sunrise. Then the lamp is taken and hung at the uppermost point and lit as dusk falls. You then place the other instruments and perform the usual actions as before then meditate on the new structure. The final banishing is by the hexagram ritual which will be always used from now on.

Between now and midwinter you can repeat this operation any time between the hours of sunset and sunrise as convenient. Just for this first year no Daytime magic should be performed until the following equinox -

this is to emphasise and clarify the difference and avoid confusion. The other task is to obtain or make a gong and Drum and decorate them for consecration at Midwinter.

At Midwinter (ie when the Sun enters Capricorn around December 21st) you prepare the temple for Midnight, leaving your old Disk off the altar. Just before midnight you enter the temple taking your Drum and Gong which are placed on the altar. The banishing hexagram is performed just before midnight, then the statement is made "it is my will to consecrate this Drum and Gong". They are placed at the Midnight point with the words "with this action I consecrate the Drum and Gong". They may be struck once or twice, but no serious drumming should take place during this ritual, because that belongs in Summer day magic.

Between Midwinter and Imbolc you continue to practice as before, but with the Drum and Gong in place of your old disk. The emphasis should be on meditation, but you can also practice using the laser torch to trace sigils in the night sky.

At Imbolc (ie as the sun enters 15 degrees Aquarius around 2-7 February) you prepare to perform the ritual at Sunrise with the statement "It is my (our) will to confirm the structure of Winter Night magic". Note that this ritual runs into daylight, albeit Winter daylight, just as the Lammas one runs into dusk. This shows that there is flexibility to perform winter magic by day, or Summer day magic in later winters. The categories are not rigid, except one would probably avoid the extremes of performing Summer magic on a Winter's night, or Winter Night magic on a bright summer's day. The only exception to this rule could be at the two solstices where the rules could be broken as a Feast of Fools celebration. This is more likely to be a Winter Solstice event: when a crazy drumming ritual takes place as part of a midnight Saturnalia revel.

Between now and the Spring Equinox you decide on a new form of Dagger to suit your approach to the new magic. You make it and prepare to consecrate it at Sunrise on the Spring equinox (ie as the Sun enters Aries). This is done as before with the statement "it is my will to consecrate this Dagger to the Great Work", and the Dagger being placed at the Sunrise point after it has marked out the tetrahedron. Purists might insist on using the old dagger to mark the tetrahedron, because the new one is not yet consecrated, then the old one could be stuck into the Earth (after asking Earth's permission) to mark its retirement.

From now on one is an initiated magician of the new trinitarian non-tradition, a pioneer of the new aeon. One of your first acts should be to use the dagger to carve a triangular lamen to be worn during rituals as a mark of this honour.

POSTSCRIPT

I have presented myself with a problem.

It was never my intention to tell you more about the resolution of mine own inner yob/gent duality, because 1) I do not assume it is any of your business, 2) I do believe that this book is of less value if it gives all the answers and does not present problems that demand your participation in some measure, and 3) I think there are already too many pop psychology books padded out with personal case histories.

On the other hand I feel burning, passionate love for anyone who has taken the time to read my words, and I want to repay such attention by providing the very best value possible. So I will carry the story forward a year and a half, but hedge it about with caveats.

The rage simmered away over the months: mostly quite negligible, occasionally bubbling up. Then there came a period when it seemed to build up more persistently as if trying to attract attention. I found myself fuming over folks who steal cars then set light to them so that they are not only no further use to the owner but also a burnt-out blight on the countryside. This image seemed to be persistently bubbling in my mind, and the usual process of "just imagining what I would do if I caught the buggers at it" no longer seemed to relieve the pressure.

So I hit on the idea of taking this further. It occurred to me that people who step outside of normal life become easy game: if you murder someone on their own territory you risk being seen or noticed in many different ways, but if you murder someone who is engaged in unlawful activity they are already partly invisible, and you have far greater chance of getting away with it.

At this point I felt uneasy. Until now my imaginings had been really just play: daydreams of "just imagine what I would do if I caught the buggers at it" really amounted to masturbating away my rage. But now I was serious: I decided to plan the perfect murder, as a sort of vigilante exercise where I could catch gangs setting light to cars and kill them and leave their bodies to char in their burning cars. I made myself plan this in great detail: how to catch them, how to kill them, how to destroy evidence and how to evade detection. Against my own distaste (for my rage had already subsided) I pitted a sense that I was putting across a message to something inside me. I went over the plan very carefully to iron out any loopholes, then I waited for a response from my unconscious (or my demons, as you will).

The next morning I awoke from a dream that I was back at college. I went back to my old rooms and found they were now occupied by a Holy Man. I suddenly felt anxious because there were police there and it dawned on me that I had murdered someone last year and almost forgotten about it. I turned away and began to take evasive action to outwit tracker dogs etc. But my anxiety grew because I realised that it was one thing evading the police, but quite another to evade the Holy Man who would be able to read my mind, even at a distance. Then I woke.

The dream felt like an urgent message as I woke up. Then I realised that it had a trinity of characters: Holy Man, Policeman and Yob. I use the word "Yob" for the character of the murderer in the dream because I had forgotten about the murder, so it must have been a mindless amoral act rather than an act of intense passion or malicious, thoughtful planning.

What had happened was that the "Gent" had split into two characters: the Policemen and the Holy Man. The Holy Man was a wise figure with vision, but he could be ineffectual. The Policemen was an upholder of society and order, but he could be dogmatic and unfeeling. The

Yob was a source of energy and excitement, but also arrogant and amoral.

Violence lay in both the Policeman and the Yob, but in different ways. The Yob liked to beat people up merely to enjoy the power over them, to be "one up". If that meant they ended up dead, too bad. He didn't particularly *want* to kill. It was the Policeman who could have a real intention to kill, and it came from his strong moral sense that unsavoury elements should be eliminated for the greater good.

Contemplating this trinity I realised how it had been lurking behind my life for as long as I could remember. Like any trinity that is not recognised and treated right, it could collapse into duality in several ways (compare my earlier example of Love/Hate/Indifference).

When the dynamism and thrust of the Yob merges with the vision of the Holy Man it formed the Revolutionary. This could be a very positive character, a dynamic force for change and growth, but it meant projecting out the Policeman to create a duality in which the Policeman became the hated force of reaction, of obstinate resistance of blind, stupid dogmatism (because it now lacked access to the Holy man's vision or the Yob's sense of play). In the corruption of duality the revolutionary in turn could become the maniac iconoclast smashing everybody's comfort and security in reforming zeal.

When the Policeman and the Holy Man merged you got at best the Gent - a man of perfect manners and thoughtfulness with a strong sense of propriety. This meant casting out the Yob who now had no access to vision nor any sense of order. In this dualistic corruption the Gent could be replaced by the Nazi, who was the Policeman inflated by the Holy Man's vision until utterly convinced of his divine moral right.

When the Policeman and the Yob merged you got at best the Soldier - arrogant energy disciplined for the national good - or at worst a real "Bent Copper", the type that would beg to be given the job of evicting hippies for the pleasure of cracking a few long-haired skulls - (for hippy read Holy Man in this scenario).

All three of these dualities were ones that used to make me boil with rage. Again, I remind you that I am not talking of righteous anger but the sort of passionate rage that tells us that somewhere in the system a thermostat has gone on the blink. The sort of rage that seems immensely powerful but is actually pretty impotent.

I have felt a big shift in me after that dream, a good shift. But here is the caveat. Don't get the simple notion that finding the third principle is an immediate remedy, a magic potion. That would be to elevate the third principle into a superior position to the original duality by calling it "the solution". Remember what was said about false trinities: the real thing is truly balanced, a horizontal equilateral triangle. The real healing does not come as soon as you find the third principle, but only after you have lived with it and got used to it until it is an equal member of the team.

Imagine a word association test: someone says "God" and you reply "Devil". The resolution is not when you read in this book about the Trickster, but when you become just as likely to reply "Trickster" as "Devil".

Another message for those looking for simple solutions: a few days later I had another dream which raised a whole new issue related to this one... But now I will stop writing, for you have no need to know about that!

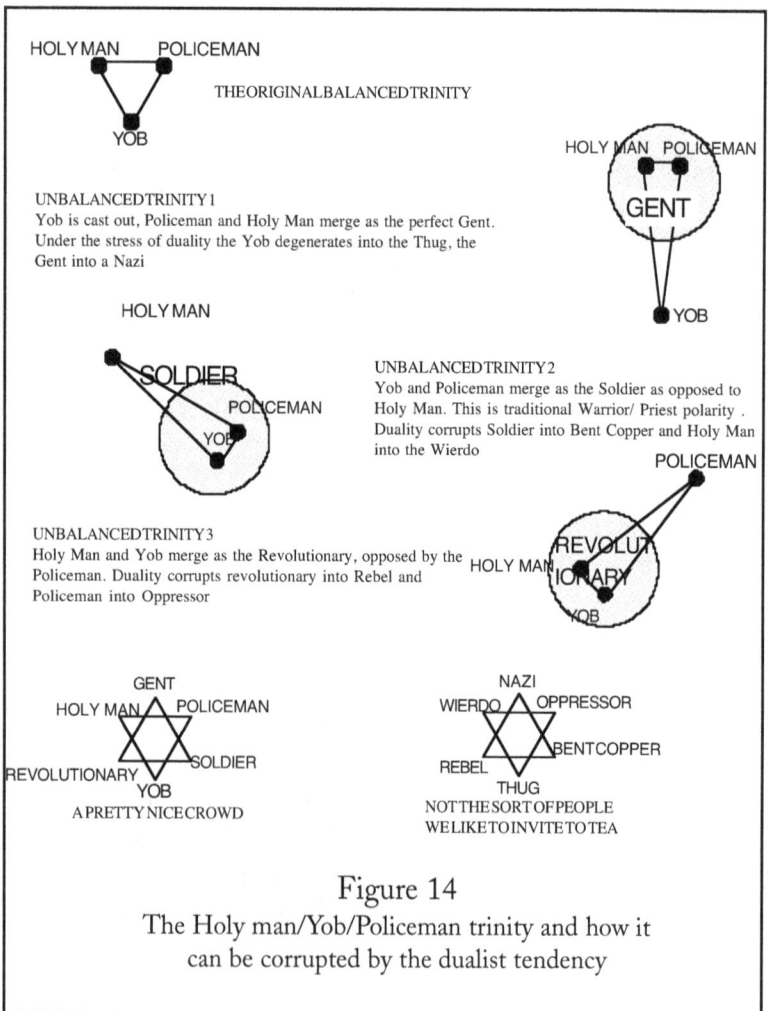

HOLY MAN   POLICEMAN

THE ORIGINAL BALANCED TRINITY

YOB

HOLY MAN   POLICEMAN

GENT

UNBALANCED TRINITY 1
Yob is cast out, Policeman and Holy Man merge as the perfect Gent. Under the stress of duality the Yob degenerates into the Thug, the Gent into a Nazi

YOB

HOLY MAN

SOLDIER

POLICEMAN

YOB

UNBALANCED TRINITY 2
Yob and Policeman merge as the Soldier as opposed to Holy Man. This is traditional Warrior/ Priest polarity . Duality corrupts Soldier into Bent Copper and Holy Man into the Wierdo

POLICEMAN

UNBALANCED TRINITY 3
Holy Man and Yob merge as the Revolutionary, opposed by the Policeman. Duality corrupts revolutionary into Rebel and Policeman into Oppressor

HOLY MAN

REVOLUTIONARY

YOB

GENT
HOLY MAN   POLICEMAN

REVOLUTIONARY   SOLDIER
YOB
A PRETTY NICE CROWD

NAZI
WIERDO   OPPRESSOR

BENT COPPER
REBEL
THUG
NOT THE SORT OF PEOPLE
WE LIKE TO INVITE TO TEA

Figure 14
The Holy man/Yob/Policeman trinity and how it
can be corrupted by the dualist tendency

AFTERWORD

ooooo

A CONFESSION

ooooo

THE ENDING OF
THE QUEST

My name is Adamai Philotunus, philosopher of Glevum, for I have indeed had my fill of twoness. Weary of battles and knavery I set forth on my quest to find that true elixir in which all dualisms would dissolve and find their solution.

Four great rivers have I braved, calling out for those who would follow me. Each river lead to this dark ocean now before me, seething, sultry, mysterious. This is where the true discovery begins. I have an urge to look back to see who is following me, yet I know that could prove fatal as it did for those travellers who found their way back from Hades. I have sounded my message, to find now that I am alone might break my remaining resolve.

So dream on, Philotunus: imagine that the world is with you, eager for example. Apply your birthright, as a son of the Ram with the Archer on the horizon, and look only ahead, careless of what lies behind. Step forward.

The water surprises my feet, caresses my ankles. Some remains of paint is dissolving - little matter for it was a thin disguise. Most would already have recognised behind the mask of Admai Philotunus one Ramsey Dukes the Spinning Mouse.

Yes, it is I, Ramsey, who edges forward into these saline depths. Is this to be my final solution? Readers may have divined the simple formula of my writings: to take some common and accepted duality and turn it on its head. If the world insists that white is black, Ramsey Dukes will argue that white is white merely to flaunt the arbitrariness of it all. Thus he was ever a player of dualities - the spirit of the Trickster himself who fled knavery only to discover the Knave. That is the Deux of Ram Sea Deux. But before us lies the Sea.

I entered the body of a young man to be a medium for my message. I chose an able bodied scholar of pure mathematics at the University of Cambridge, a competent rower, an inventive artist and not without some mastery of words. This surely must have been my recipe for success, so I settled like a tongue of fire on his brow.

Now, twenty four years on, I ride a tired old hack with few remaining grey hairs. He has the soul of a yuppie yet is middle aged, poor and downwardly mobile. My ideas are like a fever in this weary brain. He coughs them out like snot. Has he failed me or have I destroyed him? So much he wanted to do in life, and all he has to show is a handful of self-published booklets.

I should therefore depart, release him for his sunset years in peace. My limbs are flowing away. My eyes are running. Is this ocean no more than my tears?

So Ramsey Dukes bids you "hail and farewell".

God be with you.

Goddess be with you.

The Child Horus and the third aeon of Information be with you.

Glug.

THE END

APPENDICES

APPENDIX A
HIGHER NUMBER SYSTEMS

The book has majored on trinitarian thinking, but has also done reasonable justice to certain other number systems: namely one, two and four. What it has not done is examine five-fold or higher systems. This appendix intends to repair that omission.

To do so it will begin with an apparently outrageous assertion, then proceed to defend that assertion, and finally conclude by considering a few higher number systems in the light of that assertion.

The assertion is this: *there are no higher number systems than the quaternity.* It may seem an outrageous claim because it seems to deny such well-known systems as the five Chinese elements, the seven-fold system of the Theosophists, the ten Sephiroth of the Kabbalah and the twelve signs of the Zodiac.

So let me now justify my position.

This is a pretty quirky book. I am interested in a particular sort of reader. A reader who walks past the big high street bookshops and seeks out the obscure and arcane. The reader who ignores the bestseller lists and looks for hard-to-reach shelves labelled "miscellaneous" or "other authors". A reader with a savage hunter instinct that is drawn greedily to the piles of spineless little self-published pamphlets for which no sane bookseller allows shelf space.

For this reader I have laid a veritable minefield of disincentives: an unheard-of author from a cranky publisher; ludicrously extended latin sub-titles that say "this is

going to be hard work"; absurd cod-alchemical introduc-
tions; academically unrespectable personal references
and pages of magical ritual mumbo jumbo.

No weedy academic nor fundamentalist moral
cripple has a chance in this wild treatise. We are now acting out the climax of the film: I, the evil mastermind am
skulking in my battle HQ when - in a shower of broken
glass - the surviving reader bursts in. Anyone who has
persevered this far must be an *ideas animal*, a Stallone of
the psyche or a spiritual Schwarznegger with bulging
moral muscles, a belt laden with hi-tech critical weaponry and every sense fine-tuned for signs of danger.

I reach out to embrace this blazing-eyed philo-
sophical fiend that has tracked me thus far against all
odds. For that minefield was no defence, but rather a test-
ing ground. I want readers who are *better* than me for the
task that lies ahead.

For the number systems I am writing about are
active at very primitive levels of the mind. I wrote earlier
of the most humble numerical system among the most
backward people, of the system that knows only three
numbers: one, two and many. In this system "three" stands
for all higher numbers. My belief is that dualistic thinking lies at that sort of level of our unconscious minds. At
a level with very little idea of higher numbers. In Jungian
dream analysis the number four has a very sacred role: it
appears as the four-fold cross or *mandala* and represents a
sort of spiritual completion or ideal. Now I believe that
this special significance is because the number four lies
beyond the comprehension of that part of the mind: it has
only evolved to the point where the number four means

"the great infinity beyond". And it cannot even handle a real three-dimensional quaternity, or tetrahedron: it can only present the number four as a double duality or two-dimensional cross because that is the limit of numerical understanding at the level where duality rules.

So the quest to establish trinitarian thinking demands hard work. It is not a question of "I've just read this amusing little book and have decided to think in threes from now on", but it is a question of negotiating the deepest inner jungles to educate the savages there.

I also believe that these natives already have some experience of the trinity - witness its appearance in alchemy, astrology and the myths of the three-fold Goddess. But they have not, for many centuries been *encouraged* to think that way. Certainly not to communicate such thoughts.

Now I want to recruit inner Rambos to this task not so much for their brutality as for their courage to face the wildest jungle. For what is needed is encouragement as much as any cracking of the whip. We will be airlifting supplies and sustenance and... music please... *love* to those parts of the brain that show signs of adding the trinity to their mental armaments. Encouragement is truly needed because we are actually *stretching their minds*. To do this we need the courage to get down to that level and to co-operate: this is because psychology as well as politics has moved on since the nineteenth century: we can no longer relate to the wild natives of the unconscious as their superiors, just as we can no longer negotiate with third world countries from an arrogant imperialist standpoint.

Now you may see the sense in which I claim that no higher number systems exist. When I look at apparent higher number systems, I find that they always seem to be sub-divided to help with their assimilation.

The ten-fold system of the Tree of Life is usually analysed as a series of "triads": the number ten is translated into three triads and an appended Malkuth. I believe that this has to be done to make the symbol work at these deepest levels, to be more than a clever mental construct.

The seven-fold system of the planets also tends to be analysed into sub-sections: The two Luminaries, the two Inner Planets, the three Outer Planets; or the Sun as centre to a hexagram of three pairs of polar planets - Moon/Saturn, Mars/Venus, Mercury/Jupiter.

To illustrate this in greater depth let us consider the numbers five and twelve.

FIVEFOLD SYSTEMS

Whereas the hexagram splits naturally into two triangles, the pentagram is a unicursal figure that at first seems solid, and surely well enough established to qualify as a traditional system of thought - Figure 1.

But as soon as I draw the pentagram I am caught up in a dualistic problem: for tradition insists that their are two pentagrams. The *upright penta-gram* has one point upwards and is a traditional symbol of Good, whereas the *averse pen-*

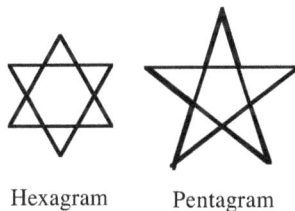

Hexagram   Pentagram

Figure 1

223

tagram has two points upwards and is a traditional symbol of Evil - Figure 2.

Why is this so? Some say that the pentagram is a symbol of life because it represents the four elements of matter completed by the super-element Spirit. This is

Upright   Averse

Figure 2

shown as in Figure 3. So the averse pentagram is naughty because it elevates Matter over Spirit, whereas the upright pentagram places Spirit in the supreme position.

All this talk of "Matter over Spirit" is, of course, utterly dualistic and it shows how our comprehension of the pentagram is bound by the duality inherent in directions: the symbol is conceived as if on an upright page. If it was viewed as a horizontal symbol like our perfect equilateral trinity, then words like "over" and "under" simply wouldn't apply. But what we are in fact seeing with the pentagram is its subservience to duality: the five is divided into two, namely four elements of Matter plus Spirit.

Spirit

Fire   Air

Water   Earth

Figure 3

This is not the only way the five is divided. The number five was a holy symbol to the Cathar christian sect. The pentagram featured as a major symbol in their churches - and this might explain why certain christian fundamentalist bigots still revile all forms of the pentagram, upright or averse, as evil. God's love was manifest to such christians as a papal decree that anyone who slaughters a man, woman or child Cathar not only had all their past sins forgiven but also all future sins too. (A useful sort of decree for a church that wants to get the Mafia on its side.)

Now the Cathar religion, for all its pacifism, was also highly dualistic. They believed that this material world was a creation not of God but of the Devil. To me this suggests that at some level they saw the pentagram not as five equal points but as an upper Divine Trinity and a lower Diabolic Duality. The three upper points represented the Spirit or Kingdom of Heaven, while the lower two points symbolised our duality-torn world of flesh.

Now the last of the Cathars was sacrificed as a blood offering to the Pope in 1321, and is reputed to have died with the prophesy *"au bout de 700 ans reverdira la laurier"*. If we are indeed going to witness a revival of Catharism in the year 2021, then I suggest that it will have greater chance of survival if its followers carry my present labours forward and attempt to conceive a pentagram that is united and equal in its parts. If the pentagram remains divided it will be bound to succumb to the fourfold cross once more - because christian inquisitors live by the law of dirty fighting, "go one lower than your opponent".

A TWELVEFOLD SYSTEM

This has already been introduced. In the first part of my text I mentioned the astrological scheme of the twelve signs of the Zodiac and how it can be analysed as four groups of three. Thus twelve is broken down to four times three, where four stands for the four elements and three for the Cardinal, Fixed and Mutable qualities.

Crowley, in his book on astrology gave good advice to those who wanted to familiarise themselves with the Zodiac by guessing people's signs. He told us not to go straight to guessing signs, but rather to take it in two stages: first guess the element, then try to decide on the quality. This was a recognition of the point I made at the beginning: it is hard for our minds to analyse in higher numbers, so reduce the process to no more than four categories and it becomes much easier. So, rather than try to guess "Aries" in one jump, you say "a Fire sign for sure" and then "not so much Leo or Sagittarius as Aries, I reckon".

This 3x4 division leads to a rather neat symbol system that I will expand on here because it can be used for the drum in the New Magic system.

Taking the three dimensions of space to represent the three qualities, you can define a cube which has twelve sides corresponding to the twelve signs - Figure 4. Now this cube has six faces, grouped as three opposing pairs - a natural symbol for the six planet system.

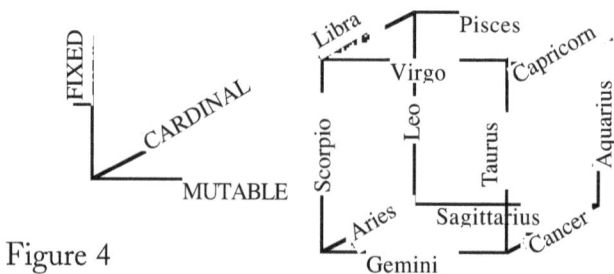

Figure 4

It also has eight vertices which can be made to represent the eight trigrams of the I Ching. The most logical way to do this is to split the cube 2x2x2 to give eight cubelets representing the binary system of taoism extended in three dimensions to give the eight trigrams - Figure 5. If this cube is rotated and represented isometrically in two dimensions you get a plane hexagonal figure as in Figure 6.

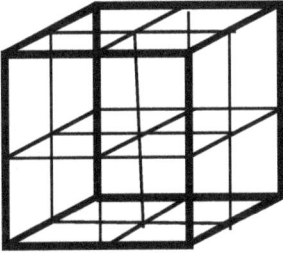

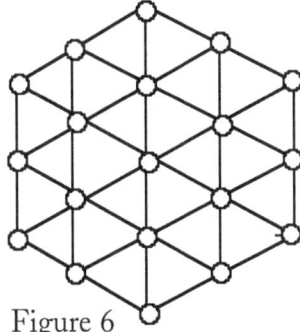

Figure 5   Figure 6

In this representation you note that two of the cube's eight vertices are superimposed at the centre: if the cube is oriented correctly these can be the Yin and the Yang trigrams and can be represented by the traditional Yin/Yang symbol at that central point. The other six trigrams are represented by the six corners of the hexagon. That leaves twelve further crossing points on which the twelve signs of the Zodiac can be drawn according to the cube's edges. You also note that the figure is made up of twenty four triangles: so that the twenty four runes of the Elder Futhark can be drawn in these spaces.

This is the symbol that I drew on my drum for the trinitarian magical working. It is a single glyph that unites the symbolism of the I Ching, the Runes, Astrology and Alchemy.

A magical operation is realised on such a drum by using its symbols, together with a number-symbolism of beats, to represent a question or intention. "I want to cre-ate a slogan for a revolution" could be analysed on the astrological scheme as one beat on Aries for the fertilising idea, followed by two beats on Gemini to represent man-ifestation in words, ending with four beats on Aquarius (representing Uranus) for crystallisation in revolution as outcome. "How can I increase my income in my present career?" could be represented by a finger pressing on Capricorn to fix that point of the drum skin (Capricorn representing the tenth house, damped to represent a fixed point) while beating a single invoking stroke on Sagittarius (representing Jupiter as increase) and a double manifesting stroke on Taurus (representing second house as money).

As a magical act one would attempt to maintain that same rhythm with utter concentration to the point of exhaustion; as a divinatory working you try to maintain it but allow the hand to wander as trance develops. You then observe where and how the drumstick now falls and inter-pret the symbolism for a suitable answer.

If I manage to weave photographic images into my software you will be treated to a Figure 7 illustration of this drum. Otherwise probably not.

THE CYBERMASS OF THRICE GREATEST DATA-HERMES

This ritual was performed at a Chaos Magick Conclave at Lockenhaus Castle in Austria in 1990 as culmination to a series of talks I gave on the theme of this book. It was designed to mark the initiation of a threefold vision of reality, where information could take its place alongside matter and energy as the fundamental elements of existence (see my book "Words Made Flesh"). On a more spiritual plane, the ritual was also designed to provide a bundle of laughs for all present.

Although the main emphasis in the ritual is trinitarian, it also incorporates unitary, dualistic and four-fold symbolism in order to bed the "new" thought securely on established principles. There is a strongly Hermetic trickster element too: this was underlined in the original performance by the early explosion of a glass candle holder which cast shards across the floor where we would be dancing barefoot, so the rite had to be interrupted to clear the damage. Ho! Ho! Nice one Hermes!

The Materials

I had used a tetrahedron of the elements in my talk, as described in Part Three. It stood about a foot tall and consisted of four shiny aluminium rods entering four brightly coloured spheres of Fymo, which was flourescent and glowed interestingly under ultra violet light. So I also had a small battery UV lamp - as used for reading secret flourescent writing on domestic goods one does not wish to be stolen. This latter was not vital to the ritual, but part of my "tricksterish" effects (such as gadgets to create mysterious flashes of light) added to amuse Hermes and invite his participation. I also intended to create a large tetrahedron (aligned as for Summer Magic) in the temple, made of six three-yard ribbons anchoring the vertex on an overhead chandelier. I cannot remember if this eventually happened, but the duality of the greater tetrahedron in which the priest stood and the smaller one on the altar was intended as a Microcosm/Macrocosm symbol.

The chamber was an East/West oblong, and in its centre stood an altar, centred on the altar was the large tetrahedron, on the altar stood the small one.

There were four brightly coloured trays - red for Fire, Yellow for Air, Blue for Water and green for Earth - and fixed to each was a fire bowl (little metal bowl containing glass wool soaked in alcohol). I wanted to make the flames of the same colour as the trays, but could not get the effect I wanted so made do with alcohol flames. The trays were filled with water, partly to balance symbolism, partly as a safety measure, and partly to ensure that the process of handing them round would be a delicate and tricky task - as anyone who has handled a wide shallow dish of liquid would understand.

On the altar stood also a large candle, a pot containing the sacrament, and a number of small disposable bowls in which the sacrament would be distributed. For the sacrament I chose those curious mixtures of seeds provided as a palate freshener by some Indian restuarants. The idea was to find something non-harmful and yet mysterious and unfamiliar on the tongue. The fact that it was made of seeds seemed symbolically appropriate for the seeding of a new way of thought; the fact that the mixture contained a distinct taste of lavender seemed appropriate to Hermes.

Other items included a fire wand (I used a conjuror's vanishing flare to add a nice trickster effect), drums, a smoke making machine, strobe light and a powerful hi-fi tape system.

I refer to two sub-rituals: the banishing Lesser Pentagram and the Lesser Hexagram. The former is very well known and is given in countless magic books, so I will not describe it here (anyone who has never come across it should not be performing the Cybermass anyway). The latter is less well known, so I will describe my version of it adapted to trinitarian magic.

The Lesser Hexagram Ritual

The original lesser hexagram is a fourfold ritual based on the traditional cross of the elements, and is meant to follow the pentagram ritual. But few people use it as such - why? My own theory is that it does not fit well in the four-fold framework as it is essentially a three-fold ritual, so people tend to find it a bit feeble and unmemorable compared to the good old rock solid pentagram ritual.

But this version brings out its trinitarian feel and, to me, works much better. Hence my suggestion that the hexagram ritual would *replace* the pentagram in trinitarian magic, and one would only use the pentagram in cases such as this where one is forming a bridge between the two systems. As such we would use both invoking and banishing hexagrams, and we would allow the extension to the Greater Hexagram Ritual as (inadequately) described in Crowley's Magick In Theory and Practice.

I should warn you at this point that some people who do use the traditional Hexagram ritual say that it's role is to banish the "higher" elements, as opposed to the "lower" elements banished by the Pentagram. I respect this opinion as an interesting and realistic recognition of the fact that true purity requires not only "evil" to be banished but also "good". As such it could be used to argue that I should not be using the Hexagram to replace the Pentagram in my magic, but for my own part I believe that this trinitarian magic contains its own resolution of the Good/Bad or Higher/Lower dualities and so requires only one banishment, and for that the hexagram proves ideal.

Note that, although INRI contains four letters, the first and last are the same, as when circumscribing a triangle (this point is illustrated in part four figure 10). The word "ARARITA" is made of the initials of a sentence in Hebrew which means "One is his beginning, one is his individuality, one is his permutation" - an expression of the threefold AUM (Cardinal, Fixed, Mutable) formula.

1) Stand facing Noon point (for Summer/Day magic, Midnight Point for Winter/Night magic), feet together, left arm at side, right arm holding Wand (eg drumstick or torch) upright at the solar plexus

2) Vibrate:
    "I N R I
    Yod Nun Resh Yod
    Virgo, Isis, Mighty Mother
    Scorpio, Apophis, Destroyer
    Sol, Osiris, Slain and Risen
    Isis, Apophis, Osiris
    IAO"

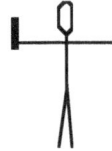

3) Extend arms and say "The sign of Osiris slain"

4) Move to swastika stance and say "The sign of the mourning of Isis"

5) Move to V stance and say "The sign of Apophis and Typhon"

6) Move to X stance (arms crossed on chest) and say "The sign of Osiris risen"

7) Moving through LVX stances say "L, V, X. Lux. The light of the trinity"

8a) *SUMMER/DAY MAGIC*

With wand trace hexagram of Air (see Figure) in the Sunrise point (defined in Part Four) while vibrating "ARARITA"

Trace hexagram of Fire in South while vibrating "ARARITA"

Trace hexagram of Water in Sunset point while vibrating "ARARITA"

Trace hexagram of Earth overhead while vibrating "ARARITA"

| Hexagram of Fire | Hexagram of Earth | Hexagram of Air | Hexagram of Water |

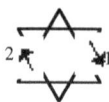

The four invoking hexagrams, showing first side and initial direction to draw the first triangle, and the first side and initial direction for second triangle. The banishing hexagrams are identical in shape, and begin at the same side , but the direction is reversed.

8a) *WINTER/NIGHT MAGIC*

With wand trace hexagram of Water in the Sunset point while vibrating "ARARITA"

Trace hexagram of Earth in North while vibrating "ARARITA"

Trace hexagram of Air in Sunrise point while vibrating "ARARITA"

Trace hexagram of Fire overhead while vibrating "ARARITA"

9) Repeat 1) to 7)

THE CYBERMASS OF THRICE GREATEST DATA-HERMES

The participants were asked to divide into three groups: Cardinal, Fixed, Mutable. The basic division was by sun sign, but if anyone strongly identified themselves with another sign, they could choose accordingly. That gave me three roughly equal groups. The form of the ritual and their respective roles were described and rehearsed in advance.

We entered the darkened chamber and sat in meditation while ominous music played. I chose William Bolcolm's "Black Host", the long introduction which I faded as the central electronic bit was about to begin. Then the Priest lit the central candle and thus broke the darkness. This was the signal for the Cardinals to rise and stand in the East, the Mutables in the West, and the Fixed folk to form an outward-facing circle in the middle of which I gave the statement of intent "It is our will to initiate the trinitarian magic" and proceeded to perform a thunderous OTO version of the banishing pentagram ritual.

Note: those present were Chaos magicians, and they later said how they liked the way this ritual combined very formal, impressive elements with the chaos elements.

Cardinals started drumming and the Mutables chanting. The drumming at this stage was not rhythmic but rather an excitatory pattering sound of fingers on drums. The Mutables were given the highly dualistic chant "Behold the sight of Light in flight before the might of Night" and were told to make it as dirgelike and hypnotic as possible. They were also told that, in keeping with the trickster spirit they were free to subvert the chant by reversing the words "Night" and "Light" if they felt so inclined. In practice, with a non English-speaking crowd, they soon forgot the words and made a curious yet satisfying droning sound.

The Priest handed the four trays to people at four quarters of the Fixed circle, then lit his torch from the central flame and circumscribed the circle, lighting the four fire bowls in turn, starting at East and going deosil. The Fixed circle began passing the trays round the circle deosil.

This had an element of ordeal: passing trays filled with water and containing fire-bowls in the dark around an outward facing circle requires great concentration, especially with the Cardinals pattering and the Mutables droning away.

Meanwhile the Priest vanished his flare and performed the invoking Hexagram ritual. As the flames died down, any Fixed who was handed a tray where the fire went out had been told to smash the tray outward to the floor. Thus we all heard four crashes.

On the fourth crash the drumming and droning stopped and the Fixed circle turned to face the centre and linked hands. The Cardinals began a slow and purposeful four-beat rhythm to which the Fixed performed a "pace, pace, bob, bob" circle dance, marking three directions: inwards, sideways, outwards. To do this you stand in a circle facing inwards and holding hands. Starting with right foot you take two forward steps towards the centre then bob twice; take two sideways steps to your right and bob twice; two backward steps and bob twice. This is continued ad lib.

Here an element of challenge or competition was introduced: The Cardinals had a duty to provide a good rhythm to stabilise the dance, but they also had to slowly accelerate the rhythm. The Fixed had a duty to maintain the dance as perfectly as possible for as long as possible, while the Cardinal aimed to speed it up to the point where the dance became chaotic.

Meanwhile the Priest was focussing (in word and movement) the triune energy into the sacrament on the altar. As the motion without grew more and more frenzied, he slowed down, breathed deeply and grew calmer.

When the dance was close to breaking point, the strobe light came on and smoke began to be generated. When the dance pattern broke down, the Fixed group broke out of their circle and everyone was dancing crazily and freely throughout the room. They were told to dance ad lib till exhaustion, when they should collapse on the floor. Fixed and Cardinal were told to fall outward to the walls, the Mutables to fall inwards so they were closest to the altar.

When the last drum had gone silent and all was still, the Priest waited in silence until the moment felt ripe, then began distributing the sacrament in little bowls to the Mutables with the words:

"I bring the seeds of an new understanding, of a new overcoming, of a new inspiration."

They take the bowl and reply "Information is my substance, Information is my becoming, Information is my being". They then place a few seeds on their tongues and begin chewing them.

The mutables spread out, passing the sacrament to all present, until all have partaken. Each recipient repeats the formula and takes a few seeds. All sit in meditation, chewing the seeds until all flavour has departed. Curious quiet music was playing. When it finished, all arose and banished with laughter according to the Chaos tradition.

Note: it had been explained beforehand that this was a Hermetic trickster ritual where cheating had its place. Those who did not accept my information model of the universe said the same words but with different meaning. If they preferred the materialistic model they were saying "in Formation" (meaning "in formation (noun) or matter") instead of "Information". If they preferred the energy model they were saying "in Formation" in its verbal or energetic sense meaning "in the act of formation".

During the ritual the mental state of the Priest was interesting. It evolved slowly along these lines:

"Oh God, what a shambles, I wish I had not made this so complicated!

Why the hell have I lumbered myself with all this conjuror's trickery and gadgets? It means I have to concentrate so hard, while I far prefer to get lost in a ritual and play it from my heart. Here I have to keep a cool head, now where was I?

The participants don't seem to be aware of my panic, that's good. At least I can concentrate on my act and play it up a bit: let's wow them with ultra-dramatic gestures and thunderous intonation!

Crikey! They seem to be falling for my act – thank heaven I cannot see how stupid I must look – here goes!

This ritual is totally bogus, I am faking the whole thing and the punters seem to be lapping it up – lets make a flash of light appear as I raise my hands – pow! nice one.

Hey! I get it! I really am in the ritual! This 'act' is actually me being taken over by the Trickster! I am indeed playing the Charlatan Magus role required by the priest. Ok, then, let's really give 'em the works!"

After the ritual, during which I had felt utterly "cool", I was told that it was a brilliant experience for all present. The Trickster had indeed been present. The banishing laughter was long and loud.

239

APPENDIX C

IN PRAISE OF DUALITY

It goes against my principles to repeat material overmuch between volumes - in the way that compilation albums in the sixties used to be designed to include just enough new songs to induce you to purchase, but enough old material to make them cheap to produce.

This following essay has already appeared in Volume III of my collected essays "What I Did In My Holidays", so I need to justify my repeating it here.

It is, of course a good principle not be enslaved by principles, but that is only a personal triumph and not one that will benefit the reader. It is also interesting to consider how this same essay might appear in a different light in a different context. As in that Borges tale about the man who rewrote Don Quixote word perfect, I can imagine the academic world one hundred years on being split into two irreconcilable camps: the one insisting that this essay as it appears in this volume lacks the subtlety and scope of the original in "What", and the other insisting that the original is no more than immature ramblings compared to the towering intellectual achievement shown in Appendix C of this book. (So now you know my phantasies!)

Far greater justification, however, is that this essay is highly relevant here. It is, in a sense, an essay in praise of dualistic game-playing and, as such, it provides an excellent balance to the trinitarian emphasis in the rest of this book. Although I have repeatedly stressed that I am putting forward trinitarianism as an important addition to rather than sub-

stitute for other systems of thought, our inherited dualistic bent means that it is easy to forget this and see the book as a battle cry for overthrowing duality.

Just as we needed the discovery of duality in order to gain a real appreciation of unity - remember my early example of how a society never feels more unified than when it is at war against a outsider, and how internal wrangles creat a yearning for unity - so also will the discovery of trinity lead to a better appreciation of the game of duality. Again an earlier example: if we were completely inside the game of chess, so that each captured pawn felt like a soldier killed or limb torn away, then the game would be hell and it would have degenerated into paranoid defensive play; but in fact we stand outside the game as "players" who dive in and out of the situation for a combination of excitement and a chance to reflect. Thus the duality of chess becomes a delight and an art.

You still find people arguing that the way to heal duality is to regain the peace of inner one-ness. This view overlooks the fact that we first chose duality to escape the limitations of that one-ness. The so-called "problem of evil" would be much easier to solve if it was only poverty and deprivation that lead to crime: however, the child brought up under ideal conditions of comfort may well choose to rebel and drop out from its "bourgeoise" upbringing. It may even become a drug addict in persuit of something "beyond". For, as it says in the Book of The Law, "I am divided for love's sake".

A retreat to one-ness may deliver temporary relief to the individual, but it does not heal a duality. Thus I hope that the lessons of this book might lead eventually to that maturity of trinitarianism that would allow us to return to our old dualistic addictions and battles and rediscover amusement, delight and eternal scope for play therein. This Appendix explores ways in which this could happen.

As to the change of context: one useful point from What I Did may be lost in this placement. This essay points out that the view among less thoughtful Christians is that "worship" means total subjection to a deity, and it is this viewpoint that makes the idea of devil worship abhorrent. I suggest that this is a decadent view, and that there is more sense in the pagan or primitive view that worshipping a deity meant forming a right relationship with that deity - so that the worship they perform to evil spirits is not the same as that performed for good spirits. The "right relationship" with your local mafia boss is not the same as the right relationship with the vicar (unless they are the same person): whereas it is morally forgivable to insist as a personal stand that no relationship with a mafia boss is "right", it is far more dubious to preach that view to others, because it is tantamount to preaching suicide. Now, in the other book I suggest that this unthoughtful Christian view is a degenerate one because it is a symptom of the age that Crowley described as the aeon of Osiris - a sort of childhood of mankind where we tend to project ideas of perfection on our parents and gods. But we are now entering his Aeon of Horus which is more like the adolescent phase typified by arrogance, defiance against gods, disillusionment as the image of perfection crumbles, and yet a necessary step toward becoming adults or gods ourselves. If you cling to the idea that God is utterly perfect, the only possible worship has to be total subjection. If you lose that divisive sense of perfection (and if you survive the loss), then worship can become more an act of co-operation.

IN PRAISE OF DEVIL WORSHIP

Thinking back to a couple of earlier essays which, as it were, "probed the naughty bits" of occultism, this looks set to become part three of a trilogy. So I'd better start by going over some ground already covered.

The black magic article (ghost written for Hugo l'Estrange) published in Chaos International, looked at the popular notion that "black" magic was magic for evil ends, whereas "white" magic was done with good intention. It was suggested that that was not a very useful concept, because who the hell does magic seriously for evil ends?

The most evil people I could think of - certain nazis, inquisitors, witch hunters - all saw themselves as servants of the light. It was not inconceivable that someone somewhere might consciously dedicate themselves to pure evil (rather than just saying that to shock the grown ups) but such dedication would be so pathological as to seem really rather sweet - certainly not a major world movement to be seen as pitted against the beleaguered forces of good.

I suggested that the only meaningful distinction seemed to be in the means rather than the ends: black magicians were those prepared to work with, and on, more sinister forces. Such work is dangerous, but it can be very necessary for the health of society.

This point will be expanded in the present essay.

The article on Satanism, to be published in Fenris Wolf, began by trying to sort out the confusion between Satanism and the subject of this essay - Devil Worship.

The analogy I drew was between the confusion of "communist" with "revolutionary" in our society,

Because I personally value ideas over facts, I always saw a clear distinction between the words "communist" and "revolutionary", whereas those who value facts over ideas would equate the two, saying "you show me ten commies, and I'll show you ten revolutionaries". Nowadays I can support my viewpoint by pointing to what is happening in the Eastern Bloc where communism is no longer revolutionary: it is the norm, and positively reactionary. In other words: the popular idea that all communists are revolutionaries has more to do with living in a capitalist society than it has to do with the practice of communism. Not only is the idea not universally true, it also leads to a lot of polarised hysteria.

Similarly with Satanism: because Satan can represent a polar "opposite" to Christ, and because we live in a Christian society, anyone wishing to worship the Devil will tend to equate Satan with that role. The result is a distorted picture of Satan and what Satanism stands for: a viewpoint responsible for a lot of polarised anti-occult hysteria, and yet an understandable viewpoint in a Christian society.

The distinction was drawn between Satanism and Devil Worship so that I could go on to talk sensibly about the former. I did not wish to launch a new polarisation in which Satanists formed a crusade against devil worshippers in order to "wash their hands" of this bad association. Moral hand-washing of this sort strikes me as pernicious, and I drew a comparison between self-righteousness and squeaky-clean lifestyles.

It is possible to live a squeaky-clean lifestyle, with not a speck of dirt or wear in your life, but it is very difficult to do it without creating a mess for someone else to clear up. It means regularly buying new cars, chucking out any furnishings that get marked or scratched, buying your food hygienically wrapped and preferably precooked... and so on. The result is a mountain of garbage which lands on someone else's doorstep.

Not only does someone else have to dispose of or re-cycle that garbage, they also have to endure social rejection. Like flies on shit, there is something psychologically unsavoury to squeaky-cleaners about those people (eg gypsies) who live off society's garbage. The squeaky-clean lifestyle survives by creating a pollution problem, and an underclass which is needed to re-cycle that problem.

The moral analogy is with those who deny all but their cleanest principles: they generate a moral pollution problem which has to be projected onto a despised minority.

Take for example the principle that Christ's sacrafice means we need no longer offer blood offerings to the Gods. Yet surely the biggest religious sacrafice of all time must be the tens of millions of turkeys which are slaughtered in the name of Christ every December?

Liberal Christians recycle, or at least learn to live with this particular bit of moral dirt because they are prepared to face up to and come to terms with this incongrous pagan survival in their religion. But whiter-than-white fundamentalists refuse to see it: instead they create the notion of an evil pagan minority who perform animal sacrafices. Many pagans, faced with this moral garbage being dropped on their doorstep, opt to become vegetarian animal rights campaigners - yet they remain a despised underclass to the fundamentalists.

So the point of this rather long introduction is this: the following essay is a further attempt to recycle some of the moral garbage created by extremely self-righteous elements in our society. It is not an attempt to wash our hands of that garbage.

The Polarity Game

Imagine you are interviewing a nanny for your toddlers. The first candidate bubbles with sweetness and light, laughing at your jokes and saying how lovely your children are, the weather is, the garden is... The second launches into a diatribe about the evils in our society, about child abuse, ritual murder, pornography...

Which gets the job?

Now I know that jaded old decadents like myself will soon weary of sweetness and light, but nevertheless, if choosing a companion for children of a tender age, I for one would be distinctly unhappy with the second candidate. I would value the positive messages of the first candidate more highly than the protective anger of the second... unless I was myself feeling highly insecure.

By the same token, I am very wary of organisations who claim to cherish children, but who spend a lot of time talking to the media about the hundred and one most horrible things you can do to them.

I am a great respecter of the power of human imagination, and would challenge anyone to a contest as to who could devise the sickest way of disposing of noisy neighbours' children en mass. But, having taken my prize, I would go home for cocoa and an early night.

As I write this there is probably somewhere in the world a lonely psychopath flipping his lid and sharpening an axe - anything is possible, I once saw a Volkswagen break down - but all the same, how can anybody seriously believe that there is a great worldwide conspiracy of organised evil, hell-bent on the ritual abuse and sacrafice of children? I distrust any household that leaves that sort of moral garbage in its dustbin.

Just ask who these ritual devil worshippers are meant to be. We are assured that they have infiltrated every level of society. Let's forget tabloid hysteria and ask ourselves what we are being asked to believe: namely that *real* people are involved in ritual child sacrafices.

How do they manage so many undetected crimes (the police know nothing of this conspiracy)? How do they dispose of the bodies? Can you picture them at breakfast the next day? "I hope you don't expect *me* to clean up the blood in the temple *yet again?*" "Sorry, darling, I must dash or I'll be late for the board meeting".

Alas, I have to make it sound commonplace, because we are being asked to believe that it is commonplace.

This is the image of devil worship being projected by some groups: not only do I find it impossible to believe in, I also feel very mistrustful of the people who do believe it. Nor would I want to leave any children in their care.

Occultists are accused of secretly practicing these evil rites. But what is their motive meant to be? If there is no motive, then the behaviour is pathological and we should see its practitioners as sick people needing healing. That attitude does not suit the campaigners, because they want to call the public to arms; so the onus is on them to create a motive so they can paint the evil as a deliberate evil, and yet they cannot come up with anything credible.

The problem is this: whereas occultism has nothing to gain from encouraging the vile practices described, fundamentalist christianity has everything to gain. According to its rigid interpretation of the scriptures, Antichrist has got to set up his kingdom of evil on earth in time for the year 2000. Unless evil becomes rampant throughout society as predicted, these predictions will be blown... and fundamentalist christianity will have to retire with egg on its face.

Of course I am not seriously suggesting that individual christians are deliberately conspiring to cause a breakdown in our society in order to make their religion come true - that is almost as hard to believe as the devil-worshipper myth - but I am pointing out how declining morality and mayhem are exactly what fundamentalist christianity needs for its survival.

This is an idea I discussed in Words Made Flesh: how any group can function as a system, developing a group-mind or artificial intelligence which can often act against human interest. I gave examples like the medical profession - high minded folk who generate work for themselves by implanting negative health suggestions on cigarette packets; the Tories who came in on promises to restore law and order, yet have produced change after change in society apparently designed to fragment society and create public disorder - because the group mind of Toryism knows that happy folk are more likely to opt for socialism, whereas frightened citizens will vote for tough government; similarly, every action of the legal profession is a perfect vehicle for creating more work for itself.

The trouble with our western scientific world view is that it has banished the idea of "spirit" or mind in anything other than human form. This revolution has, up till the present, lead to great technological advance but the bill is about to be presented: the West will now have great difficulty in coming to terms with artificial intelligence, whereas the world's more animistic cultures will see nothing extraordinary in the idea that a machine or even an abstract system could have a mind of its own. Technology is about to outgrow the mind of the Western culture that created it.

So what I am saying in these examples is that it is not Mrs Thatcher's deliberate fault that everything she does serves to increase violence in society, rather it is the fault of a system called Thatcherism which needs violence for its survival. Otherwise well-meaning people become part of an artificial-intelligence which acts against human interests - not because the system is inherently evil but simply because it is a primitive entity which puts its own survival first.

So we see that fundamentalist christianity, as a system, needs to generate evil to feed itself. Comfortable people are notoriously irreligious and this produces the paradoxical fact that non-political secular institutions tend to increase world harmony whereas religious and political movements tend to decrease world harmony. To observe these effects you have to change your focus: don't listen to the motives of the people involved, simply concentrate on the final outcome.

In my Satanism article I gave the example of a woman who appears in the media saying how she was involved in a satanic cult that sacraficed animals and children - and now she is a born-again christian who travels the country campaigning against evil. But if you consider her motives for joining her satanic cult, it can only have been to gain power and position - which she now has, as direct consequence of her seedy past. So the seductive message to children which lies behind her public attacks on Satanism is this: if you want to be a media star like me, do as I did, and at least pretend that you have made sacrafices to Satan!

Polarised thinking seems terribly clear cut and black and white when you are engaged in it, but it seems equally ridiculous and muddled to those who can step outside its framework. We see Christians campaigning against the evils upon which their very faith is founded, we see forces of law and order provoking disturbance to stir up justification for their existence. Who has really benefitted from the Poll Tax? the answer has to be... the Labour Party.

Anyone who has ever strongly opposed a government in power must have known that feeling of elation on hearing about exceptionally bad employment, inflation, trade or other such figures. Your eyes are set on the dream of a government's collapse, and you see yourself as a "good guy" because you are opposing a bad government. But you do not notice that you have got into the habit of praying for your country to get into a crisis - a crisis that will get the "good" government into power at the expense of the nation's immediate health - and what sort of good guy is it that wishes ill of his country? As the Duke of Wellington kept pointing out: victory is the second worst thing that can happen to any campaigner.

There are an infinite number of polarity games: good/evil, black/white, rich/poor, right/left, revolution/reaction, liberal/totalitarian, christian/pagan... But each game has exactly the same rules and they are just different names for the one game called "God/Devil".

The God/Devil game is played on a map of the world painted in only two colours. The rule book says "nothing could be simpler than a two colour map".

However, today's *confit de canard fumée* will be tomorrow's shit. And the perpetrator of this foul alchemy is not Satan, nor the Commies, nor the drug barons... it is our own bodies.

Her Majesty the Queen, Margaret Thatcher, His Holiness the Pope, and Mother Teresa all have something in common. Every day they sit on the loo and leave a smelly brown deposit for the sewage workers to dispose of. If it is "bad form" to acknowledge this fact, what about the people who actually perform the act?

The God/Devil game may be played on a map of only two colours - black and white - but it not at all simple, because the boundaries on that map are fractal. Any cross section of that map contains as much black as white: wherever you slice it, you find God and Devil locked in eternal embrace.

If you take an information model of reality (as discussed in my Words Made Flesh), the polarity game is analogous to deciding that the number one in the binary system is good, and the number nought is evil. In theory there is a "perfect' program whose machine code contains no zeros because it consists entirely of ones - but, like a perfect God, it doesn't actually do anything.

Devil worship is simply the recognition of one's right to change sides in the polarity game.

The Nature of Worship

Where has our society got the idea that to worship something is to subjugate yourself to that thing? That to worship the devil is to become his slave?

If you are in the polarity game, two things conspire to stop you changing sides. One is the conscious belief that, whereas the service of God is perfect freedom, as soon as you bow to the Devil you will be enslaved. The second is the unconscious knowledge that, once you have changed sides, you will in fact find that nothing has changed (this is because the game is perfectly symmetrical, if it were not so it would not be a proper fair game). You do indeed discover that you are enslaved, but not to the Devil so much as to the game itself.

Other cultures seem to recognise that worshipping spirits can at least bestow a measure of power over them. Their concept of worship seems somehow more sophisticated: it is the act of establishing a right relationship with a deity.

The current myth of devil worship is that it means going from total dedication to the Good to total dedication to the Evil. This myth is the moral equivalent of a nuclear deterrent: it is designed to make devil worship, like war, unthinkable. Such techniques merely appear to succeed: we find other names for war so that we don't have to think about it as we continue to pursue it, and the sheer unthinkableness of devil worship means that we are free to practice it forever - but unconsciously. Tell a militant labour supporter that he is helping to keep Thatcher in power, or a fundamentalist christian that he is romanticising the occult, and neither will know what you are saying.

The animist who consciously sacrafices to an evil spirit in order to keep it out of mischief is playing the polarity game in an altogether more sophisticated manner. Who is playing whom?

I remember a scene in Lawrence of Arabia where the hero is trying to win some local ruler to his side. The ruler says, with pride, that the Turks pay him money to keep out of their way. Lawrence replies that it is normal to pay servants, and when is the ruler going to stand up against his masters?

What an intriguing reversal: to what extent are we subject to the tax man, and to what extent is he indeed our civil servant? At some metaphysical level it must be true that the terrified shopkeeper who pays protection money to the Mafia is in fact reducing the latter to servitude - and the thought cheers me up. It could explain why Mafia hit men and pimps are so vicious towards their sources of income - deep down they sense how they are growing dependent on them.

So the idea that a relationship with a devil means slavery to the devil is itself just part of the game. It is as if Freedom were to appear in person and say "I alone am Freedom, if you so much as turn your gaze from me for an instant you will be enslaved and never more free." Some freedom.

In the black magic article I gave an example of a changing relationship with a demon which served to illustrate the difference between white and black magic. It was of a student who suffered a demon in the form of a nervous breakdown, who went to the college psychiatrist who was able to analyse the demon as an Oedipus complex or whatever, and thus it was banished and the student went on to pass the exams and become a successful member of society. This I saw as the epitome of white magic: a wicked demon has been banished, and a person has been liberated.

But then we reach a mid-life crisis: the hero has achieved wordly success and reputation, but somehow there is no magic left in life, it all seems pointless. At this point a different sort of shrink appears (probably far more expensive) who argues that, when that demon was banished, it took life's magic with it. Now the hero has to start a journey into the unconscious underworld to locate that banished demon and come to terms with it in order to re-assimilate its power. This I saw as the epitome of black magic: to work with evil forces instead of banishing them.

To argue that it is really white magic, because the intent is to re-cycle the evil into something good, is to miss the point horribly: anyone who approaches such work with the crusading spirit of a white knight going down to "rescue" underworld nasties and convert them, is doomed to fail. Such work means getting one's hands very dirty for a while: like the underclass who recycle society's physical garbage, you can expect to lose a few friends and supporters during the journey.

That illustrates a major black magic operation or, in the terms of this essay, a bit of really serious devil worship. It shows that the fundamentalists are at least right when they say that devil worship is dangerous, but it gives perhaps a clearer picture of the nature of the danger. Certainly, devil worship is best left until one has plenty of experience of life: the devils that tempt the innocent aren't worth worshipping anyway!

But, as was suggested earlier, most relationships with devils are far less conscious - the fundamentalist who subtly tempts children by romanticising the occult in order to attack it, the politician who runs down his country while trying to gain power to help it - such relationships are also dangerous, but in a different manner. The demons are just as "bad", but the relationship is different.

In both cases the devil is being given something. The earlier example is of someone who gives the devil the gift of recognition and respect, and hopes to win something of its power in return. This is a bit like laying out food offerings to a wild creature with a view to taming it a little. The later examples are like people who pay protection money: the unconscious deal that the fundamentalist has with the devil is that he will go round building up the devil's reputation by preaching of his power and omnipresence, in return for being disassociated from that

255

evil. The devil is happy to let him live that squeaky-clean image, it generates ever more garbage elsewhere.

So the point I wish to put is this: If there was a little more honest, conscious devil worship in our society, there might be rather less of that dangerous unconscious collaboration.

The Practice of Devil Worship

To worship a devil is to turn to the polar antithesis of what you stand for, and to form some sort of conscious relationship with it.

My emphasis on the conscious element is intended to make the definition more useful. Although I see the fundamentalists as the chief supporters of their devil, I would not want to call them worshippers of that devil because it stretches the term too wide.

Devil worship, in these terms, still covers a wide field. Using the fourfold analysis of human endeavour into Religion, Science, Magic and Art (proposed in "SSOTBME - An Essay On Magic") we see that devil worship can be a powerful and risky business in the first (Religious) case. The more perfect and good is the God you worship, the more absolutely evil must be the Devil it excludes. Devil worship in the Religious sense is what we consider "real" devil worship, but it is an act of dedication so outrageous as to be very rare. Apparently St Secaire held a black mass in the crypt of his church in order to purge it of its sin - sounds like a saint with a sense of humour!

In the Science sector, the devil equates with untruth. Here devil worship is at its silliest, because it amounts to investigating ideas which "cannot possibly" be true. The danger is of being ostracised by the scientific establishment as a crank, the possible reward is that one might just hit upon some revolutionary new truth which the establishment will eventually be forced to accept. This hardly ever happens in this absolute sense: instead of serious devil worship, the scientific establishment is prepared to allow limited congress with minor demons, dubious hypotheses on the fringe rather than out and out falsehood. Mathematics seems like one glaring exception - the subject makes big advances every time a good mind is prepared to lay down a new formal structure on axioms forbidden to earlier structures - but such mathematics is more at home in the Art sector, as we shall see.

In the Magical sector the devil equates with unbalance or division. Here the dangers are most subtle: in a sense unbalance is fundamental to every effective action, and the sword of analysis is never omitted from the magic circle whatever scoffers may suggest. But you do not work long with unbalanced force without losing your own innate balance, and then becoming dependent on further unbalanced work in order not to fall over. And the skill of the sword is to learn how to control it: for if analytical reason is allowed to run wild it inevitably performs the greatest magical operation of all, namely to banish all of life's magic and leave us with logical positivism.

The next section of this essay will look further into the magical potential of devil worship.

In the Art sector, devil worship definitely has its home. This is no doubt why art never totally loses its sense of the subversive.

To illustrate I take an example from the world of advertising and image. By the late eighties commercial artists had perfected the sharp, crisp and clean lines of the "hi-tech" style, and you can just imagine some designer after a hard day with the fine-line pen wandering home past a second hand book stall and picking up a some tatty copies of a magazine from the fifties. Suddenly he bursts out laughing and shows the magazine to a friend: "hey look at these adverts, aren't they *horrible!* Look at those cut-out heads with those ghastly toothy smiles! It's so bad... I love it".

For the sheer outrageous kitsch of it he creates a fifties-look ad campaign. In fact it is worse than the original because it deliberately plays up the "bad" design. Yet out of this blatant act of devil worship emerges a new spirit: advertising looks back to the fifties and discovers some of the excitement and optimism of the decade which had been lost in the pursuit of eighties cool imagery. (Ok, they then ruin it by flogging it to death, but that's because they are working for wallies.)

This devil worship is so common in the arts that people would not recognise the term. But if you can imagine that sense of gut-excitement felt by each artist who rediscovers some "forgotten" style which has been repressed by the current aesthetic conventions, and if you can identify with that feeling of "devilment" when the resulting art-work is first presented to a shocked public, then you can see that "devil worship" is an apt term. And you will understand why conventional people distrust artists.

If you can also admit that this process of fishing in the sewers of the rejected can bring up some very tasty catches, then you will see why this essay dares to be in praise of devil worship.

The Essence of Devil Worship

In the amoral world of Art, then, we see the essence of devil worship most clearly.

Some natural quality or function is repressed, cast out, or exiled. It can be a taste which goes out of fashion, an old religion which is forbidden, an emotion which is repressed, a habit which is denied. It is now considered to be "bad".

Being thus cast into the wilderness, it does indeed become "bad". Firstly it is cut off from the civilising influence of the solar conscious mind, and this means it reverts to nature, becomes wild and feral. So far it is not necessarily bad in any absolute sense, it has just lost its respectability.

The real damage to its nature comes from the extent to which it is hunted and baited by society. Perhaps the reason why Art devils are less dangerous is because they get off the lightest: they are simply treated as today's "bad taste" and are mocked and jeered at. The devils of politics and religion are far worse because they suffer extreme persecution, torture, alienation and threats of hell fire and damnation. Like dogs which not only are allowed to run wild, but are also beaten, baited and hunted, they learn to bare their teeth and snarl.

259

Such maltreatment might lead to extinction, but the survival instinct is strong in the wild. Such devils grow strong because they are persecuted: they learn tricks of survival and camouflage.

Two things can then follow. On the one hand they can learn to prey on the civilised world, returning in the shadows to raid consciousness' dustbins as it were. Thus we find the Christian devil growing big on the garbage hurled at it.

On the other hand, their very ferocity can mean they now have something which the civilised world needs or wants. This is where devil worship comes in: you want to catch the wild horse for its very wildness, you want to revive Victorian bad taste for its very outrageousness, and so on.

This is where devil worship grows out of being a way to make the best of a bad job, and becomes a positive aim.

Take the example of the fanatics who sacrafice turkeys to Christ with their eyes closed, then march out to hunt for evil pagan animal sacraficers. Meanwhile the pagans, with their intense respect for life and death, have either become vegetarian or else make the cooking of meat a very conscious and solemn sacrafice. They acknowledge that life has been given that they may flourish, and they accept that responsibility with a dedication to live the ensuing life to its fullest. By consciously facing up to the carnivore in their makeup, they serve to domesticate it and render it less dangerous.

But what happens if they are confronted by the christian fanatics in battle? Might not the civilisation they have brought to their hunter-spirit have rendered it weaker than the feral blood lust of the fanatic? They have the advantage of wisdom, but they have lost the advantage of ferocity. The fanatic who denies the hunter god in himself has turned it into the equivalent of a pit bull terrier: a useful creature to have with you in battle. The fact that it is likely to turn on its master after the battle is small compensation to the pagans who are slaughtered meanwhile.

This is, to me, the most profound dilemma of liberalism. In the terms of this essay a liberal is one who has the courage to acknowledge society's demons and work on them: rather than call the murderer "inhuman" and demand his death, the liberal is more likely to recognise the murderer as "all too human" and therefore to seek ways to reform him. Keeping to this one example, what happens if the liberal comes into conflict with a non-liberal? Whereas the liberal's "killer" instinct has been partly civilised - for honest (as opposed to hypocritical do-goodery) rehabilitation work on killers serves always to temper one's own killing instincts - the non-liberal's killer instinct is a raging beast ("inhuman" and so cut off from civilisation), so the non-liberal has violence on his side and is liable to win the fight and dismiss the liberal as "woolly and wimpish".

The reason that liberals do indeed survive, as suggested in another essay I wrote on the subject, is partly because there are limits to their ability to face human "evil". Whereas the liberal can assimilate the unhappy, drunk or ill-educated person who resorts to murder, few can tolerate the "cult of violence". One only has to read Guardian articles on dog-fighting or bare knuckle boxing to get a whiff of the "macho violence for its own sake" demon lurking in the liberal unconscious. That I suggested was why - contrary to the myth that liberals are gutless - two of the roughest, meanest war machines of all time were totally rubbed out when they declared war on the liberal establishment in 1939.

These examples do suggest that there could be an advantage in having demons for the power they can supply, and that the power is greater when the demons are more "evil" and uncivilised. So now we have three phases of devil worship. At one extreme the unconscious servitude to a devil as practiced by fundamentalists - where you deny a quality until it builds explosive power which can be unleashed on your opponents, but which is liable to turn back and destroy you in the long run. At the other extreme there is the liberal approach which acknowledges those demons, goes into the wild and takes steps to tame or domesticate the beasts - a very worthy and perhaps ultimately superior approach, but it does raise the fear that something may be lost when a wild demon is tamed. The third approach is an attempt at compromise: it is to keep our demons reasonably wild and powerful while striving to develop a relationship which destroys neither party.

This approach seeks an answer to the plea "please, can't we have a permissive society AND keep that lovely exciting sense of sin?". It is what I will call "magical devil worship".

The Varieties of Demonic Experience

Again we look at the Art sector for the easiest, lightest example. When members of the art world (whether painting, literature, music, fashion or whatever) decide to cast out a style, they do so with quite perverse viciousness. Yesterday's styles are not allowed gently to wither away or be pensioned off, instead they are driven out with the whips of ridicule in a way that looks like appalling silliness and bad manners to the non-art world, to whom it epitomises all that they dislike about "trendies".

A fashion editor who was raving about "today's more demure line" last year will come out with some totally over-the-top statement like "*no-one* will be seen wearing those *awful* frumpish long dresses this season" - a statement not only exaggerated but also untrue, for simple observation will almost certainly reveal a majority of long dresses remaining in the streets. It is as if the fashion editor lives in a phantasy world with only a minimal bearing on real people in the street - but I suggest that the fashion world (as a system) is actually demonising old styles to further their power.

In the example given previously of the return to fifties advertising, it was the sheer awfulness of the imagery that gave it its magic. And the awfulness of the imagery (which was after all once high fashion) was generated by the early sixties "cool school" so vigorously and scornfully rejecting all the corny, toothy smiles and greased hair of the fifties.

The harder the art world hurls away its old fashions, the harder and more excitingly they will bounce back later. They are, in effect, creating demons to worship for their own pleasure and excitement.

A second example extends the field further, it concerns one of the great clandestine love affairs of our society: the relationship between the avant-guard artist and the bourgeoisie. Here are two groups of people who, left to themselves, would by their nature tend to die of frustration and inertia respectively. Instead they create devils of each other and give life meaning: the avant guard artist is now a valiant rebel against the forces of hypocricy and inertia, while the bourgeoisie becomes the champion of decency and traditional values.

I was upset to hear of a recent lawsuit which might make it illegal for an artist to shock the public, and I wondered if this represented an inspired raising of the stakes in a game that has grown a little tame of late, or was it merely an incredibly insensitive decision by a legal system that is out of touch with human needs? To deny shock to the readers of the tabloids would be to remove their one and only motivation; to condemn artists who provide such shocks would be as silly as to pretend that it is hatred which inspires children to rebel against their parents rather than love which is seeking recognition.

Illustrations of such loving shocks are bound to be too personal to touch many readers, so I will offer just one. Like the majority of sensualists I am fascinated by nuns: how anyone, given such a delightful plaything as a female body, could sacrafice it to a life of celibacy and fleshly mortification is wonderful beyond my ken. Now, their very lifestyle excludes me from expressing this deep affection by direct means, so instead I channel my love into a phantasy. It is that of a very prim and proper Mother Superior arriving early in her chapel for a service only to find that it has been taken over by a great crowd of naked male and female body builders engaged in a really mega-hunky group-sex workout.

Now when I tried out this story on a religious acquaintance, they felt it was somewhat insensitive. They did not seem to appreciate that, far from being insensitive, I momentarily *become* that Mother Superior and feel the electric frisson of shock at the sight of the altar and its furnishings crushed beneath the sheer invincible mass of grunting, moaning, pumping meat, and knowing that no attempt to go ahead with the service and invoke God's aid would have any effect on the hormone-crazed participants in this reproductive tableau. Within me, and within her, the black and white of flesh and spirit become fragmented over and over in endless layers: a dull game of but two colours becomes a fractal tapestry of unfathomable profundity and endless meaning. In glimpses of ecstacy I know and understand the nun.

Were I a painter I might portray the scene, as a poet I might put it in words, best of all it would make a splendid cinematic experience... and I would await condemnation from the catholic church, a condemnation which I would recognise for its inner meaning: that of a clandestine lover returning my affection by an outward display of contempt.

So notice how Art, with its lighter handling of demons, produces the more charming and likeable examples of devil worship, but as we reach beyond the world of Art to impinge on other areas stronger feelings are aroused. This supports my thesis that there is greater power if we goad our demons to become more "evil". The world of politics and religion produces more powerful, effective and controversial examples. Here we see the process best if we consider how a system becomes a devil worshipper - even though the individuals in that system are unaware of what they are doing.

The Nazi party gained its prominence by creating a devil in the form of a Jewish Communist Conspiracy that was uniting the world against Germany. It worshipped that devil by building up its outlines in words and pictures and films until it stood clear and menacing before the German electorate. Naziism gained enormous strength in return for this demonic pact, and yet the exercise backfired because the demon leaked out of the triangle of art and into reality - so the rest of the world really was driven to unite against Germany.

Fundamentalist christianity, as a system, is creating an Antichrist who will establish His kingdom at the turn of the millenium. It is building up this image of a world torn by evil, of sinister occult forces, of satanic conspiracy and so on. In return for these favours the devil they are creating has given them power and support from the masses, and plenty of money and influence to build up the devil even further. But here again, they could be simply preparing the funeral of Christianity by making a devil more fascinating than themselves: on the one hand there are those who accept their glamorous view of the occult and take it up for kicks, on the other there are those spiritual souls who lose their interest in Christianity because of its growing obsessive absurdity, and they find true spirituality is now the prerogative of the occult fraternity.

Such examples show the very great power and excitement possible when you worship a devil, but they suggest eventual failure to handle such power. The real concern of this section lies in the middle ground: where the devil can give useful power without overwhelming the worshipper. So we should look at some humbler, less dramatic examples of what one might call "demonolatry' in order not to over-use the word "worship".

The media provide plenty of examples of people who, however unwittingly, evoke demons to serve their ends. The problem they face is this: how to deal with a real problem in the unrealistically short time the media allows its guests. We will imagine an example, then analyse it.

Let us imagine that there have been headlines about an anti-corporal punishment riot at some public school and so the news program brings together two people to comment on the story: one is the president of, say, Teachers Against Corporal Punishment, the other is the spokesman for, say, the Conservative Parents Group. Now it might well be that, if these two people met and got to know each other under normal circumstances, they would turn out to have a lot in common - based around a shared desire to get the best possible education for all children. The only difference might be that the former saw his job as looking for qualities in the child to draw them out, while the latter might lean rather toward the notion of imposing standards of behaviour that would help the child to express itself better as it grew up. However, in the

unnatural high-pressure conditions imposed by the program - forty seconds of verbal confrontation - there is no
time for subtlety or common ground. So what does the
Conservative say when asked to comment on the aboli-
tion of corporal punishment? Instead of talking about the
real need for every child to get the best, he speaks as follows.

"I'm sorry, call me old-fashioned if you must, but
I've got no time for these wishy-washy educationalists
who haven't the guts to say 'no' to a delinquent because
they are so terrified of reppressing its precious so-called
'creativity'".

Now it's the Teacher's turn. Instead of expressing
amazement at the educational circles moved in by the
Conservative, and wondering who these educationalists
are and how they manage to survive in a classroom if they
never say "no", instead the Teacher feels threatened and is
more likely to retort with something about the mindless
violence of the floggers and how the prisons are full of
people who have been brutalised by their parents. Thus
the agenda is set for forty seconds of polarised abuse.

What has happened is that the first speaker, aware
that he has been placed in a game situation where he has
to "win" by gaining the sympathy of the listeners over his
"opponent", realises that this cannot be done by realistic
means. The only quick solution is to evoke a demon in
order to scare the listeners onto his side, and so he calls up
the demon of crazed educational liberalism. Now I doubt
that there is a single teacher in the land who never says
"no" to a naughty child, because such a teacher would
never survive in the classroom, but there is a demon that

does exactly that (so encouraging our children to run wild and uncontrollable), and that demon lurks in the mind of every anxious parent or victim of rebellious youth. So evoking that demon gets all those people instantly on the Conservative's side.

As the Teacher has not been given enough time to banish such a popular and powerful demon, he resorts in desperation to the same technique, evoking the demon of the mindless child flogger. Note that this not only calls a lot of other listeners to his side, but it also helps to consolidate those who have already sided with the Conservative, because his remarks about prison merely help further to identify him with the demon that would release every violent criminal on the ground that they had been "wronged by society".

So the discussion is not a meeting of humans, it is simply a war between demons - and it makes no difference whether the first speaker deliberately used the tactic or whether he just slipped into that form of speech under the pressure of the moment. Demons have been evoked to serve a purpose: that of winning public sympathy under the unrealistic conditions created by the media. And as long as the media insists on such conditions, demonolatry will probably remain the best practical solution. (And note how, in the terms used above, the "system" feeds itself: encouraging the evocation of demons will encourage the sort of extreme behaviour that gives the media its best stories.)

That example spanned two possibilities. It could in theory show a positive form of devil worship, when the worshipper deliberately builds up a demon in order to use it for advantage in the peculiar conditions imposed by the media. But all too often one suspects that the technique is still resorted to as an unconscious compulsion: the speaker who wishes to make a reasonable account of his cause feels panicked by the interview into expressing an extreme viewpoint. So, as in the case of the fundamentalist christian who rails against Satan, it is often the demon who is pulling the strings and spreading its own influence via the media.

The next example might seem more positive and less ambiguous - but that depends upon your musical taste. Anglo Saxon protestant culture tends to make a demon out of human feeling - it is forbidden, repressed. We see this portrayed in the Hollywood ideal of manhood: when the hero returns to the ranch to find it ransacked and burnt to the ground by outlaws who have slaughtered his animals, murdered his sons, and left nothing except a video of his wife and daughters being repeatedly raped at gunpoint, then all the emotion the hero is allowed to show is a slight narrowing of the eyes - and the camera has to zoom in really close to catch it. A culture which denies nearly all human feeling in this way has nevertheless given birth to the most sloppily sentimental art-form imaginable - country music. And the fact that country music is popular in other emotionally repressive cultures like low-church Scotland and Japan confirms this picture of a faculty that has been driven down into the unconscious - or out into hell - whence it has returned in power.

That example also shows how one man's devil can be another man's absurdity - you can bet that the heart of the meanest hired gun in Texas will turn to water at the sound of "Old Shep" being sung by Grandad. It also highlights the difficulty I have with the term "devil worship". The christian anti-occultist is someone who is *serving* the devil, his actions do not match the traditional idea of a worshipper - he is more the slave to the devil he has created. But the lover of country music is typically someone who has denied his own feeling nature and demonised it for projection onto, say, Dolly Parton, and his behaviour is much more like true worship. He knows a searing intensity of emotion that is seldom experience by more expressive people who show as much emotion as they feel: true, he may go out and kill someone under its influence - becoming a suitable subject for another country song in the process - but short of that you could say that country music is an example of devil worship giving real benefits.

The next example sharpens the focus because it considers the demonising of just one emotion. Repressing sex turns it into a devil and increases both its danger and its allure. Taking my own modest sex-life as a sample I can truly say that, whereas truly relaxed and sexually liberal partners tend to offer somewhat gentle invitation to love's dalliance, the wilder ones - you know, the head thrown back, teeth bared and gutteral cries of "c'mon, you big brute, fuck me like an animal!" - have invariably come from a strongly christian moral background. Naturally, as a well-brought up English gentleman, I find difficulty in obeying the letter of such breathless demands, but nevertheless they hold a certain charm for someone who has Sun and Venus conjoined in Aries. You could even argue that the generation of such sexual fervour amounts to the one conclusive argument to be made in favour of two millenia of christian teaching.

Seen from this perspective, hypocricy becomes the saving grace of the church. The idea of monogamy would be a disaster for the human species because it would lock the most physically attractive women onto the most prosaic, workaholic men - with a resulting constant debasement of the stock. But in practice quite the reverse used to hold, as those voluptuous wives spent their daytime sporting with a succession of handsome tradesmen and college athletes. The harder the husband worked, the more idleness his wife could afford, the more time he was out of her way, and the less energy he had to dilute her promiscuous cocktail of splendid, healthy semen with his own watery oblations. Thus, although the *idea* of the "traditional christian marriage" is a human disaster, the *practice* of it became a superb eugenic mechanism for increasing the beauty and lustful vigour of the human species.

This surely is the unconscious impulse lying behind the present desire to revive "traditional values". The joy of the early sixties was not just that of sexual liberation, it was also that of a surviving sense of sin which comes over beautifully in the early Bardot films. By the seventies that sense of sin was fading, and with it the pleasure. The eighties was marked by people being greedy in order to re-capture a sense of sin (you can tell it was pathological from the way they felt obliged to flaunt their greed), but it never really achieved the magic of, say, blaspheming during orgasm or making love against a church altar.

Another approach to re-demonising lust is to drive sex into "bad" company by associating it with other still-demonic factors. For example the current euphemism for what used to be called "love making" is now "sexual abuse" - associating sex with violence has long been recognised as a way to increase its excitement. More bizarre examples exist: recently the head of Manchester police attacking homosexuality let slip some remark about people "wallowing in a sewer of their own making". Here I must consider his avowed heterosexuality as a blessing indeed, for I would not care to be bed-partner to someone for whom sex and sewage had become inseparable. Not that I too should slip into the habit of condemning other people's devils - the point is rather to congratulate those who have shown such ingenuity in creating demons to serve their pleasure, and to consider the extent to which they still manage to keep those demons under control.

Perhaps the nearest common approach to conscious demonolatry is shown by the advertising industry when it creates or evokes a demon in order to influence a public. The best examples are in pharmaceutical advertising, where evocative but medically unsound ailments like "tired blood" are introduced in order to panic hypochondriacs into consumption; in fashion goods where one flees the demon of "bad taste"; and above all in political advertising. President Reagan's copywriters created an "L-word" demon of such power that his opponents dared not call themselves liberal for fear of association. But even here we find examples of the process back-firing because people began to believe in the devil that they had created.

So it is time to return to the principles.

Polarity Power

All the demonolators or devil worshippers I have considered have taken some quality and rejected or blackwashed it to create something powerful. They have then formed a relationship with the demon in order to gain from its power. But in many cases the long-term gain is offset by disadvantages as the demon takes control.

Is this final failure inevitable? Or is it largely the result of a refusal to do the thing properly?

Have we made a devil out of devil-worship itself? In distinguishing our religious culture from the "primitive" pagan with his host of good, bad and indifferent deities have we denied the possibility of a relationship with the bad?

All too often the politician who grabs the chance to launch into a demonising polemic when a television camera glances his way, will end up making a fool of himself in the eyes of any intelligent viewer (and such do exist, now that I bought a TV set this year). Surely, a little more calculation, a little more deliberate choice and careful aim of his words would lead to better results?

True, the most *dramatic* results can follow when you surrender and allow a demon full reign - when the politician gets "carried away" - but this is not real magic and it does backfire. Better by far is the fashion world which deliberately demonises bad taste in order to revive it with greater excitement, or the more aware christians who meditate on the evils of carnal lust in order to hot up their sex-lives - because they almost know what they are doing.

What I suggest is that we might do well to rediscover the old idea that it is possible to keep demons in check by developing a right relationship with them. That "worship" should not mean subservience. Polarity is a fundamental quality in human experience: like electricity it can be dangerous but it also has power to serve us if we learn how.

Chapter 122 of Crowley's Liber Aleph contains these words:

"Now then there is an Art and Device of Magick that I will declare unto thee, albeit it is a Peril if thou be not fixed in that Truth, and in that Beatific Vision whereof I have written in the three chapters foregoing. And it is this, to create by Artifice a Conflict in thyself, that thou mayst take pleasure in its Resolution".

To those who argue that such conscious devil worship is bound to lack the fire and excitement of, say, that practiced by christian fundamentalists I would quote from the following chapter:

"Yet be thou heedful, o my Son, for this Art is set upon a Razor's Edge... It is but to pretend, thou sayest; and that is sooth; yet thou must make Pretence so well as to deceive thyself, albeit for a Moment, else were thy Sport savourless. Then, an thou have one Point of Weakness in thee, that Thought of thine may incarnate and destroy thee."

That to me is the essence of the matter. The irony is this: I am intending to write a book on trinitarian thinking as a solution to what I see as the trap of dualism into which so many of us are caught. So why am I now defending devil worship?

If we are to grow beyond bondage to duality it should not be by retreating from it, but rather by mastering and outgrowing the process. The media entertain us because they encourage silly people to adopt silly views. If this formula was simply dropped, the world would miss a lot of laughs; but if the essential gamesmanship of it became recognised it would not only allow the players to do the job a bit better, it would save them from destroying themselves in the process.

If in this and other ways we learned to recognise and respect devil worship then we could offer help to those brave pioneers who face its dangers. Who could possibly object to a swing to Victorian values as long as it was made quite clear that this was simply the necessary groundwork to a revival of sixties decadence?

As the Tories say of their health policies "if it doesn't hurt, it isn't working".

MORE FROM THE MOUSEHOLE

The following pages reveal further titles from the same author in a number of guises. They are now available via www.occultebooks.com as e-books for a trifling £3, or as paperbacks at rather more sensible prices.

❄

ALSO AVAILABLE

SSOTBME
REVISED
an essay on magic

ISBN 0-904311-08-2

"The book that put the magic back in magic" Gerald Suster

"Materialism will have many sleepless nights..." David Hall in Sothis

"A classic" Li Grainer in Gnosis

"This book made me realize I was a magician, not insane. Or at least both a magician, and insane. Great, funny, a Grimoire disguised as an essay, only 96 pages long (I like short books, and often, short women), as well as the best book to give to people if you want them to think you are smart and goofy, as opposed to stupid and psychotic. Find it. Buy it. Read it blind drunk the first time, maybe the second time too..."
'Fireclown's basic booklist' from the Internet.

SSOTBME - AN ESSAY ON MAGIC
is now
REVISED!

First published in 1974, SSOTBME immediately established itself as a seminal text of the magical revival. A thinking person's guide to the unthinkable that ran to a second UK edition, a German edition, two Polish editions and a US edition with an Austin Osman Spare print of "The Blase Bacchante" on the cover.

The book became an essential text for the Chaos Magic current, which it partly inspired. At the other end of the magical spectrum, it was a significant influence upon the later New Age movement through its clear exposition of the extent to which our world is shaped by our beliefs.

Long since out of print, SSOTBME is now available as a paperback or e-book. What's more, it has been brought right up to date and enlarged with additional commentary to over 150 pages by Ramsey Dukes (sorry about that, Fireclown!).

The difference, and the relationship, between science, art, religion and magic. The nature of magical theory - with examples from alchemy, astrology, ritual magic, Feng Shui, tarot reading and other systems of divination. A discussion of the role of sacrifice, of demons, of cyber-animism and initiation. A concise and comprehensive survey of every aspect of modern magic and its place in our world.

It's a new, definitive magical grimoire for the 21st century, and available now from www.occultebooks.com

THE NAKED, SHOCKING TRUTH BEHIND THE INTERNATIONAL SATANIC CONSPIRACY

No question was more hotly debated by the International Satanic Executivein the mid 70s than this: should they come out into the open, or should they continue to corrupt civilisation discreetly from behind the scenes?

No voice will be better remembered than that of the Honourable Hugo CStJ l'Estrange, Minister for Moral Decline and grand old man of British Satanism, arguing that the election of Margaret Thatcher was a clear signalthat his country was weary of 60s idealism and was crying out for True Evil to lead the way forward.

Because of this stirring appeal, Satanism went public - with Hugol'Estrange's "Satanists Diary" appearing as a regular column in Aquarian Arrow. No-one could deny the ensuing moral and spiritual decline throughout our society consequent upon this exercise.

In this volume we present the entire unexpurgated Satanist's Diary in all its evil glory. Here you can meet such vile personages as: Dr Sigismund Galganspiel, Minister for Absolute Evil; Miss Florence Dashwood, of the Cheltenham Ladies' Lilith Association; the Very Irreverend Dr Eival B Myeghud DSat, DipDiab, MDem Bishop of the Church of Eternal Damnation; Dr Wunlita Suzuki, Bodhisattva of the Nez School; Ernest Synner, Student Representative... and others too revolting for words.

THE HELLGATE CHRONICLES
FIFTEEN YEARS OF SIN AND CORRUPTION

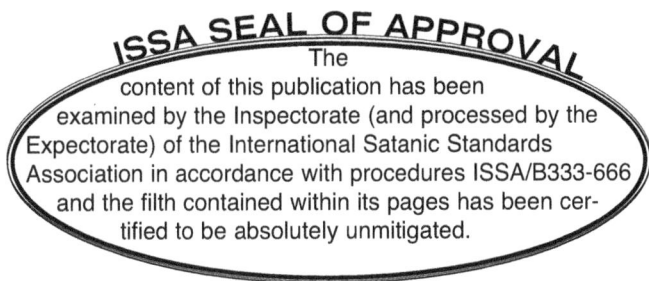

This is a DISREPUTABLE book, by The Mouse That Spins

The Mouse That Spins

A name that marks a new dawning in mankind's relentless quest for mastery of the written word.

A name synonymous with the finest in key leading-edge concepts packaged in the latest state-of-the-art Bound Off-line Optical-input Knowledge Systems (BOOKS).

A name that has transformed one corner of a bedroom in a fourth floor flat in the ancient capital of England into an International Centre of Publishing Excellence.

A name that has senior players in the world's major financial markets appearing at work dressed in mouse costumes and speaking with squeaky voices in a desire to acquire honour by association.

In short - just a name.

The Mouse That Spins' dedicated team of publishing professionals - boasting no less than fifteen man-years of occasional publishing experience between him - is proud to announce the creation of an important new imprint to head its global thrust into seminal occult niche markets of the 21st century... TMTS DISREPUTABLE.

"In presenting TMTS DISREPUTABLE to our public" explains Ramsey Dukes, Managing Editor in the European Division of the Magickal Subsection of the Contemporary Topics Department, "we aim to deploy the full weight of The Mouse's considerable financial, technical and creative resources in our determination to bring to the world a product just that little bit worse than anyone else's".

TMTS DISREPUTABLE...
A COMMITMENT TO DECADENCE

BLAST

your way to megabuck$
with my *SECRET*
sex-power formula... and

other reflections upon the spiritual path

Volume Two
of the collected essays of Ramsey Dukes

He appears more than ever a combination of Robert Anton Wilson and Tommy Cooper... The Peter Pan of the British occult scene, and long may he go on diverting us.
Paul Geheimnis, Chaos International No 15

For an unbeatable title see 'Blast Your Way to Megabuck$ With My SECRET Sex Power Formula' - thoughts on masculism, magic and the metaworld from Ramsey Dukes. Virtual Gonzo.
David Profumo, Daily Telegraph Books Of The Year, November '93

Something of Arthur Koestler, something of Loa Tzu, a pinch of Kant and a dash of Genghis Kahn - Ramsay Dukes is magnificent... Humourous, witty, written with flair and economy of style, this is certainly one of the most thought provoking and genuinely radical books I've read in a long while. If you are hacked off with old ideas and yearn for new vistas, you could do a lot worse than let Ramsey Dukes be your guide.
Julian Vayne, Pagan Voice Autumn '93

☞Why does there seem to be less magic in the modern world? *Could it be because we are all better magicians?*

☞Is it time to reinstate the Charlatan in his vital role as initiator on the occult path?

☞Is scientific thought declining in favour of magical thought, and is this inevitable?

☞Have men traditionally played a leading roles because of a deep sense of their own useless- ness relative to women? *And is this situation beginning to reverse?*

☞Might we not be living with another's virtual reality? *How would this effect our understanding of this universe?*

These and other questions are explored in depth in this volume that brings together essays written in the 1980s by one of the most original and creative contemporary writers on magic.

Open your mind to a breath of fresh air from Ramsey Dukes

What I did in my holidays
Essays on Black Magic, Satanism, Devil Worship and other niceties

Volume Three
of the collected essays of Ramsey Dukes

Is it ok for a national government to negotiate with terrorists?

Should we be prepared to make a pact with the demon Terrorism - or should we remain forever sworn to the demon No Compromise?

This is a book about demonolatry.

It was never meant to be: it began as a cobbling together of all the essays and stuff written in the last seven years. But it turned out to have a pretty consistent theme.

A theme that begins with Crowley's "Aeon of Horus" and the new, Thelemic morality. From that viewpoint demonic pacts are re-appraised: are they not a negotiation with the demonic, as opposed to sworn allegiance?

Many old and new demons lurk on these pages: black magic, sexism, elitism, satanism, publishers, prejudice, suicide, liberalism, violence, slime, bitterness, old age, war and the New Age.

These demons hold keys to power and wisdom.

They are prepared to negotiate.

Are you?

ISBN 1-869928-520
First edition, 1998, published in collaboration with The Mouse That Spins (TMTS) by: Mandrake of Oxford.
410pp Felstead 80gsm paper, stitch bound.
Now available from any BAD bookshop at £18
Or from Mandrake of Oxford, PO Box 250, Oxford OX1 1AP. UK
http://www.mandrake.uk.net

* 9 7 8 0 9 0 4 3 1 1 2 1 1 *